MATTHEW PRINCE KING

Test
of a Man

Memoirs of an Orphan Prince

Author John Gray (Men are from Mars Women are from Venus)

Test Of A Man:
Memoirs Of An Orphan Prince

Matthew "Prince" King

Dedication

This book is dedicated to my daughter Faith. As I become a better man and father, I hope that this book will put into context some of the choices I have made. I do this for you baby girl; I love you! I would also like to dedicate this book to Dr. James Maddirala and James "Yogi" Griffin, thanks for taking a chance on me Doc and thanks for always speaking this over me brother Yogi!

Table of Content

Prelude

To put my journey into perspective, I have to start when it all changed. It was December 6, 2003 and my high school made it to the State football championship game. I was excited about going to the game and sacrificed what had become the normal weekend time I would have spent with my father. Around the same time, my father was dealing with a few situations so I know he needed me around. Within the months prior, he had stepped down as CEO of his company, had been silenced from the church he pastored, and was told by my -mom that she wanted a divorce. His back was against the wall with no light of day in sight.

At any rate, my school lost the championship, so after the game I was ready to go home. I called my dad as soon as I left the stadium to let him know I was on the way. I had talked to him the past Thursday to let him know I was going to the game and that afterwards, I would meet him at our lake house. Little did I know that that would be the last time we spoke. As the day continued, his phone just rang and rang to the point that I noticed that something was wrong. That night we planned to attend a function at my god brother's job as a family. As people started to get ready for the night's event, I mentioned that I had not heard from my dad. After a while, we called a friend of the family and asked that they go out to the lake house to check on him. An hour or so past and I can still remember how loud the phone rang–we were at my brother's house at the time. My god brother's mother answered the phone in haste and I automatically knew by her demeanor that something was wrong. She told us that we needed to get in contact with my mom and that they needed to head out to the lake house… they left me there to wait.

I walked into their living room with my heart in my stomach not knowing what was going on with my dad. I tried to watch TV to take my mind off things and fell asleep in the process. The next thing I know, I heard the garage door open, and I saw my mom along with a host of other people enter the house. I could tell by their somber moods that something was wrong and then my mother leaned over to me and whispered, "Your father went to be with the Lord," and in a blink of an eye, nothing was ever the same.

Part I: Matthew
Chapter One: *The Black Kennedys*

I feel like a black republican, money I got comin' in
Can't turn my back on the hood, I got love for them

- *Jay-z (Black Republicans)*

DR. MICHAEL A. KING. As student body president of James B. Dudley High School, Michael King showed leadership that was destined for greatness. He became the youngest elected member of the Greensboro School Board. He was called into the ministry in 1978 and established Garden of Prayer Baptist Church in 1979. Ten years later, desirous to meet the ever-increasing need for affordable housing in Greensboro and Guilford County, he founded Project Homestead, a non-

Maya Angelou & Johnetta B. Cole

I have always been a dreamer. I believe to a certain extent that I am an X-man from a comic book and my superpower is the ability to dream vividly. More times than not, my dreams are the prelude to something that is about to occur in my life. When I lay down to rest, my body is still in the bed but my mind is in a completely different place. Seeing people from my past, dreaming about situations of my present and visions of the future, my dreams are the most intimate of subjects. My dream life is very fascinating.

Growing up as the son of a southern Baptist preacher, my life, like so many other preachers' kids started out in the church. What sticks out to me the most from my childhood memories are the large amounts of time I spent in church. I have seen comedians make punchline jokes about spending time in church but there was no punchline about the time I spent in the church; it was all the time! My dad was always at church doing something (i.e. marrying people, divorcing people, bible study, vacation bible school, funerals, and revivals), you get the point. Our after service schedule was an ordeal of its own; we could never just go home. My dad stayed at the church until everyone who wanted to talk to him got an opportunity.

That is just a glimpse into what it was like being the son of Rev. Michael King. He was one of the people who really believed in what he was doing and had been doing it way before I was conceived. My father was a natural born leader. He was the middle child of three boys and when my grandparents split up, he went to go live with his father. My grandfather, on his own merit, was just as interesting as my father but the two were polar opposites in many ways. My grandfather was the son of a successful root doctor who had moved his family to America from Barbados with more money than most blacks had at the time.

I remember a story that my dad told me about when he and his brother Billy went horseback riding on horses that my grandfather had bought for them. One day they were out riding trying to show off. My uncle Billy said the horse my father was riding was a headstrong horse, and that was one of the things they got a kick out of–trying to "break" horses as they call it. My dad said one day they were riding around playing cowboys and Indians and one particular time, they were running their horses towards each other. According to my uncle Billy, the horse my dad was riding had it in for him and everybody involved for that matter. As they approached each on the horses, my uncle realized that my dad's horse was no longer answering to my dad's cry to stop. Seconds later, my uncle says everybody was on the ground trying to gather themselves; him, my father, and both of their horses. My father's horse ran right into my Uncle Billy's horse causing everybody to hit the ground. Needless to say, the neighborhood kids got a good laugh at the expense of my dad and my uncle Billy.

The one thing about being a King man was the men of the family made sure you understood that we had never been slaves–only Kings. My grandfather's roots trace back to royal families in Liberia and I could tell that their mentality was a lifestyle, not just a cliché. My grandfather moved to Greensboro from Georgia with his sister and they slowly made their imprint on the City. He graduated from North Carolina A&T State University and was a captain in the Army during the Korean War. He owned a fish market, gas station, drive-in movie theater, and legend has it that he was also one of the biggest gangsters on this side of the Mississippi.

My grandfather was a big man probably around 6'2 or so with a jerry curl and was as black as they come. He lived a very flamboyant lifestyle from his women to his clothes to his cars. He was successful, and he wanted you know it. His sister Eula Vereen taught home economics at NC A&T for years and was very politically influential as a county commissioner. I remember going to her house as a child for a fish fry and remember seeing all these "political" people." Truth be told, she was actually having a campaign fundraiser for some big time candidate. As the young folk would call it, she had the "Juice."

I didn't get to see my grandfather in his prime. By the time I came around his health was failing and the IRS had come to take all of his wealth for not paying taxes; he never really recovered after that. It always amazed me how a personality like his could produce a personality like my father's. This amazed me because of how young my father was when he said he wanted to start a church. Oddly the support that his father gave him was not minimal.

I remember one story when my brother, who was born around the time my dad started his church, said that they were standing outside of my grandfather's store and my dad was trying to collect donations to start his church. My brother said that there was a drunk guy outside messing with my dad and it began to bother my granddad. After a few verbal threats, I guess my grandfather had enough of it and went outside and poured liquor on the man and set him on fire right in front of the store. My brother said it was the most awesome action-filled event he had ever seen as a child. But that's the type of man my grandfather was—he didn't take no mess, and let him tell it, his justification was that "He was a King!"

As I reflect, I understand that royalty is not dictated upon the character of a person but the bloodline in which he or she was born into. This made more sense to me from the standpoint of there had been many Kings throughout history and their reign was reflective of their personality, and in the King family, personalities were big and colorful. My grandfather gave my dad a lot of responsibility at a young age. He gave my dad a gun and allowed him to run the corner store for him. I am guessing this is around the time that my dad realized how much money my granddad was making. I remember stories about my dad saying how they had horses on Alamance Church Road and how his dad had pretty much owned the entire block of Martin Luther King and Benbow Road in Greensboro's Southside area. My grandfather bought all of his sons' houses on the same street that he lived on and had control of a majority of the business both legally and illegally flowing through the community. My older brother used to tell me that he learned how to memorize numbers so well because the old ladies would tell him to give their numbers to our grandfather if you catch my drift.

Sometimes when I run into certain people from his generation, they'd tell me about "Captain King" and how he used to have his fish market or use to throw concerts with James Brown. This was the first established King generation in Greensboro, and they made a heck of an impact. This was the start of what I understood my family to be in Greensboro. If people needed something, they came to the King family. To a great extent that is the biggest difference between my brother and me. My brother Malachi, who is a few years older than me, spent more time with my grandfather during his prime. He looked up to my grandfather and how he ran his "Kingdom." With all things being equal, I believe that it was a blessing for me not to be exposed to that part of the King's legacy. I always looked up to my father, which is the underlying difference between my brother and me, but we will get into later. The conceptualization of the generation that my father grew up in is important because it explains how he got his start especially at such a young age. It also sheds light into the chambers of his personality and what helped to create it.

My father's mother also came from a very influential family in Virginia where her mom was a very well-known educator. Today there is a school named after her. She attended Hampton University for a while and because of her "curious ways," her family felt that it was better if she transferred to the all girls' school named Bennett College in North Carolina. As I remember her, my grandmother was a very sweet person with a very fiery personality. I can see how that drew my grandfather to her. Although my grandparents did not stay together, they were able to produce three great sons who were all talented and charismatic in their own way.

My uncle Ray is a genius when it comes to chemistry. He owns his own manufacturing company and makes a lot of products from the ideas that came to his mind. My uncle Ray has a big "King" complex and has helped to instill the King legacy into me. My Uncle Ray is also one of the most righteous people I know, and I always admired him for his moral and values. I always enjoyed my long talks with my uncle… probably a lot more than he realized My Uncle Billy who was the youngest was the typical carefree jokester of the three and did not take to the King complex as much as his brothers. My Uncle Billy and Uncle Ray lived with my grandmother coming up, and I believe that is the cause of the strife that existed between the brother(s). Growing up I was never as close to my uncles as I felt like I needed to be.

When my dad started his church, he started it out of the Hayes-Taylor YMCA, in a small room on the top floor with less than 10 people for the first service. Essentially, and at the age of 19, he was given the keys to his own business–given the fact that a church is technically a non-profit. This was the start of his "Kingship" and the passing of the torch, so to speak, from my grandfather to his son. Although my grandfather was definitely not the holy type, he supported my dad. When he saw how serious my dad was, he purchased a house on Britton Street and created my dad's first church for him. My dad met my brother's mom, who was an awesome singer in her heyday. Supposedly, she is the love child of the late great Ray Charles, and I figure this to be true because of how strong her voice was. I can imagine that was one of the things that drew my dad to her. She had a beautiful singing voice and my brother does too. They had my brother in September of 1980, and my father had been a pastor for no more than a year at that time.

I can only imagine the pressures of starting a full blown family at that age with so many responsibilities, but my dad had something special about him. To be so young and to have people call you their pastor has to mean that they believe in you enough to trust you to be their spiritual guide. I can see how he and his wife at the time playing off of each other–she would sing the church up and he would come after her and preach the church down!

For some reason, they separated, and it was not a pleasant separation according to what I've heard. My brother ended up living with our dad as my dad's career kept rising. His congregation grew, and he used that to help run for a position with the county school board. He was 24 at the time, and I could only imagine where his head was about holding a public position at such a young age. But one night he was able to speak to me from the grave.

Childhood friend Nick   King Family

Chapter Two: Memory Lane

Back in the days when I was young I'm not a kid anymore
But some days I sit and wish I was a kid again

-Ahmad (Back in the Day)

I found this interview that my father did when I was in my graduate master's program one night late in the library. The amazing thing about this article is the fact that my father was twenty eight years old, and it was done right before I was born. I was actually given an insight on my father's thoughts and background from his own words. Needless to say I read this article at least ten times that night; I was so intrigued to see life through my father's eyes.

By the time I was born he had already become the mighty Rev. Michael King, and I've always heard stories that seem more like urban legends. Since I never reached the age to ask him these in depth questions, this article gave me some insight on the man whose blood runs through my veins, but I could no longer physically talk with.

KATHY CARTER: This interview is with the Rev. Michael King. Reverend King, we generally start by just speaking a little about your background, your upbringing, and then move on into subjects concerning the Civil Rights Movement and race relations in Greensboro. Are you a native of Greensboro?
MICHAEL KING: I've been in Greensboro most of my life. I'm originally from New Jersey. I grew up in Virginia. I was sort of an Army brat. So we did some traveling; extensive traveling. But I guess for the last twenty years I've been in Greensboro.

KC: Okay. So, you remember coming to Greensboro, then? It wasn't as though you came as a small child with memories forgotten. How did it compare with where you'd been before?

What were your impressions of Greensboro?

MK: Well, it's sort of hard because, you know, I was so young then, and so sort of sheltered. So, I don't remember any other atmosphere other than just a home. So, I, you know. We, like I said, we lived in Virginia, lived in California, and for a short time we lived in Georgia. We did extensive traveling. I guess I can't really make a good judgment on that.

KC: Okay. How old were you when you came to Greensboro?

MK: I would say I must have been—well, I started first grade here, I must have been around six.

KC: And so you went to which school?

MK: Miraculous Middle, a Catholic school on Lee Street.

KC: Okay. I don't know much about that particular school. I know more about the public school systems. That would have been a black school, or was it integrated?

MK: It was. It was a black school. The faculty was white, but it was a private black school, a Catholic school.

KC: Okay. Did you attend that school all the way through?
MK: I attended the Catholic school until the third grade. I started public school in the fourth grade.

KC: And at that point, you would have gone to which school?

MK: Peeler.

KC: Do you remember the transition, the difference?

MK: Very much so.
KC: Can you talk a little about it?

15

MK: Of course. My fourth grade year was the first year of integration, and it was the first year of mandatory integration. I guess it was my first experience of integration. So, you know, there were a lot of differences, particularly dealing with religion because in the Catholic school, of course, religion is incorporated into the secular classes, but not so in the public schools. It was pretty much a transition for me.

KC: Okay. In terms of both religious instruction and the integrated classes?
MK: Yes.

KC: Okay. Let's see, I forgot where I wanted to go from there, I'm sorry. [laughs]. Were you, was this the neighborhood school for you, or were you part of a busing?

MK: Part of a busing. We lived then on Alamance Church Road, so we were just within the city limits. So, it was busing.

KC: And you had to go how far every day?

MK: Across town, maybe five or six miles.

KC: Do you recall any problems, adjustments, or tensions in the integrated classrooms?

MK: I think. As I said, it was the first year of integration. I think originally, you know, that there was some tension. I think basically because of the unknown, more so than anything else. I guess about the middle of the year, the students found out that everyone's human, and we had a good teacher, and things sort of worked their way out.

KC: Okay. Were parents involved to any extent? I have spoken with some of the principals of elementary schools during that early period of mandatory desegregation, and they recall a lot of the tension didn't smooth over until parents began getting involved with things like PTA [Parent Teacher Association] and actually understanding what it meant to be part of a desegregated school system.

MK: I think I really think if the kids had the problem; I think the parents had the problem.

KC: All right. So, getting back to your experiences. So you went into the desegregated school system, and you graduated high school in the system?

MK: Yes.

KC: You graduated, I understand, from Dudley; is that correct?

MK: That is correct.

KC: Okay, then did you go to college?

Garden of Prayer Baptist Church
2020 Textile Dr. • Greensboro, NC 27405

Rev. Michael
A. King
Pastor

Bus:
(919)
272-3943

Res.
(919)
273-8903

MK: I went a short time to Guilford and to John Wesley, and that was basically a short time in both of those colleges.

KC: Going back to something that occurred to me while you were on the phone. Why did your parents send you to Catholic school?

MK: I think then it was a status symbol, going to a private school. Back then, of course, about the only private school that you could actually go to was Catholic.

KC: And your parents then were comfortable enough that they could send you there–they were prosperous enough. Was your father retired military by that time?

MK: No, he didn't really retire the military; he left the military–captain status. He opened up a service station here in Greensboro.

KC: I see. Okay. Well, that just occurred to me, and I wanted to make sure before it slipped my mind again. So, you went to Guilford and John Wesley for a while. How was your experience at Guilford?

MK: It sort of reminded me of my Catholic days–a Quaker school, it was somewhat religious oriented. It just sort of reminded me of the Catholic days.

KC: And then after you went to post-high school for a while, did you become an ordained minister?

MK: Yes.

KC: In what denomination?

MK: Baptist.

KC: Okay and you have a church here?
MK: Yes. One of the reasons I left John Wesley, I got married and ended up pastoring a church. I started pastoring at

nineteen; I've been pastoring this church for ten years.

KC: Which church? MK: Garden of Prayer Baptist Church.

KC: That's quite an interesting religious background you have. [both laugh] Catholic school education, Quaker college.

MK: And grew up Methodist, so.

KC: Grew up Methodist, and now you're a Baptist?

MK: Yes, I finally saw the light. [both laugh]

KC: Okay. And I understand that in the eighties you got involved in the school board–is that?

MK: Yeah.

KC: At the beginning of this decade. What led you to become a school board official?

MK: I was the student body president at Dudley High School when I graduated. They had started a new program that once a month the president of the various high schools met with members of the board of education. That sort of intrigued me as far as the board was concerned. But initially, what got me involved was the misplaced, the misplacing of one of the high school coaches, Jonathan McKee. He was the athletic director at Dudley High School. He had a very prominent position in the black community. And he was sort of railroaded, demoted, and just treated very horribly. To see that the board of education just refused to address it at all. They just would not address it in any shape, form, or fashion. This is what sort of ignited something in me to run. The more I got involved in that, the more I was able to see the other injustice that was going on in the system.

KC: Can you give me some examples?

MK: Well, there was a—well, we dealt with Dudley High School. There was a noticeable change in the faculty there. In talking with some of the faculty members, they were just very, very disgruntled and dissatisfied with the way they were being treated. We discovered that Dudley was always operating without resources. There were just a lot of things that once we got into the McKee case began to surface. The student ratio was changed so. When we were going to school, it was about half and half in all the schools, or at least that was the goal. But they were so warped now. At Dudley I think then was about 85 percent black, and you had Page School on the other side of town with just the opposite. So, things were just so different and no one seemed to care.

KC: And you knew for sure, you could see for sure the inequities. For example, between Dudley and Page?

MK: Yes. Yes. Throughout the whole system. One of the other things about Dudley is they had the largest dropout rate. They had the largest retention rate, they had the largest suspension rate, and it was the smallest high school. Particularly the year we got involved, it was I think 1100 students at Dudley, and there were 869 suspensions. I was just extremely concerned why the principal was allowing Dudley to fall so far behind the other schools, why she would misplace, displace, Coach McKee when he was such a role model, and always had the respect of the citizens of Greensboro. Dudley was systematically designed to close. The zoning, they changed the zoning. Dudley, the zone that fed into Dudley High School, was a mature community. You had Benbow Park and Dudley Heights—there weren't any kids coming out there because you had a lot of retirees. Dudley didn't have [housing] projects, and there are reasons for that, but your best athletes tend to come from the projects because sports were one of the few resources that they have. They spent more time in that kind of thing. So, Dudley was really designed to close. I felt that from the board level I could possibly force some changes.

KC: Okay. And you were elected to the board in when?

MK: I, I guess it was eighty—'85.

KC: Okay. So you served for a couple of years?

MK: Yes.

KC: How was it dealing with other members of the board? I would imagine—I wasn't living in Greensboro at the time, but I would imagine it would have been a predominately white committee?

MK: It was. It was. It reminded me of Apartheid in Africa.

KC: Really?

MK: Because you had a system that was predominantly black being ruled by a predominantly white board. The culture concerns and the ethnic concerns were not addressed. They saw things the only way any person could see, from their own perspective. They saw things from a minority perspective versus the majority perspective. It was extremely hard to get the board to do some things that would benefit the whole system. When you have that many—when you have minorities making up the majority of the system, then I think special concern should be addressed to the minority and minority needs. It was hard to get them to see that, such as finding role models. We had very few black counselors in the system, and consequently, we discovered the students were told that they didn't need to go to college, or if they were encouraged to go to college, they were encouraged to go to predominantly white colleges. So, it is all of these factors that keep the system like it is.

KC: Sure. What happened when you would try? You strike me as a pretty outspoken person who would speak his mind on any subject–what happened when you tried to change the viewpoint of the school board to get them to come around on some issues that you think are very important?

MK: Well, number one, their attitude and the way they dealt with problems was to ignore that they exist. As long as we pretend that there's no problem, then we don't have to worry about a solution or any of those things. It was always a struggle to make them acknowledge that there was a problem. That was just a bigger problem, an unbelievable problem, to get people to open their eyes when their intention was to keep their eyes closed to the issues. Then it was extremely hard to get them to do the right thing, to solve problems. Usually, we had to be satisfied with some type of compromise, versus getting what needed to be done to solve the problems.

KC: Sure. Can you think of an example of that?

MK: A prime example may have been the principal at Dudley High School. She–we had the uniform code of conduct, which was a policy of the board that every student would be treated, and disciplined alike. Infractions would receive punishments, and as I told you, her suspensions were three times higher than any other school system. I mean than any other high school. Initially, the administration's position was the reason her suspensions were higher was because blacks act up more. So, there were two black board members, Dr. Alma Adams, who is on the school board now, and me. We then went in and started checking the reasons why the kids were being suspended, and discovered that she had her own policy that if a student was late to class three times, it was the same thing as an absentee. The system had–it's been so long I think the figures may be wrong–I think it was five absentees out of a class, you were dropped. She was counting the tardies. Three tardies for her as an absentee, and so it added up. So, kids were actually being dropped and suspended. I think the system was after five absentees, then you were dropped from the class. After three unexcused absences, you were suspended. She was counting the late absentees, three as one unexcused absence. This accounted for why her suspensions were three times higher. And I–I mean, it was just unbelievable. It was just unbelievable the trouble we went through. What brought this on was that they had a girl who was vice president of the junior class. She was late for class a certain amount of times, and they counted the lateness as absentees and suspended her. Then there was another rule that stated if you were suspended, you could not serve as a class officer. So, they stripped her of her office. Then another rule that said that you could not be a cheerleader if you were suspended, so they stripped her of her cheerleading. All of this was brought about on this girl, and it almost just totally crushed her.

KC: And this is a nice kid.

MK: She was an honor roll student. Plus, they were counting these suspensions and other things such as if you were suspended because of absentees, then they counted the days you were suspended against the five days that you missed, then you were dropped from your class. It was the matter of the girl being late, she was suspended, she was dropped from the classes, she was stripped of her title, and she wasn't allowed to be a cheerleader. So it just—

KC: Terrible unfairness.

MK: I was forced to do some unbelievable things to even get the board to admit that the principal was wrong. The superintendent, Dr. Newbold at the time, said that he had the powers to allow one principal to run the school different from other high schools. He was citing a board–his interpretation of the board's policy. What the board did was get our attorney, which writes most of the wording of the board policy, give us an interpretation. The attorney's interpretation agreed with my interpretation. But publically, the board agreed with Dr. Newbold. So, we had a confidential letter from the board's attorney saying that the principal did not have the power to suspend, according to board policy. But the board of education refused and would not address it. They just chose not. When the question would arise whether or not the principal was wrong, they wouldn't say anything. They just wouldn't do anything. So somebody released the confidential [laughs]–somebody released the confidential letter from the attorney. They stripped me, the board stripped me, or the chairman of the board stripped me because they accused me of releasing that confidential memorandum. But I'm just saying it took all of that before the board would say, "All right, the principal's wrong." They made her rule uniform throughout the whole system. The girl was restored back to her position, and all of that. But the point was it took all of that just to solve what could have been a simple solution. So, you know, the superintendent's attitude was that blacks needed more discipline; and therefore, he was allowing this principal, which was also black, to require more from the black students. They were not even concerned about the results. Everyone knew that Dudley's suspensions were three times higher, their failure rate was three times higher, and their dropout rate was three times higher. But yet, no one was interested enough, or they just chose just to ignore that the problem existed.

KC: Or they made some assumptions about why it existed.

MK: That's right. That's correct, that's correct.

KC: Okay, you say that part of that compromise was to take that particular principal's standards and apply them system-wide?

MK: System-wide.

KC: Did the suspension rate then start to increase amongst predominantly white schools or?

MK: Yes. Yes. System-wide the suspension rate began to increase. There was such an outcry that they eventually put in in-school suspension. As long as it was just limited to predominantly black schools, there wasn't no in-school suspensions; it was out-of-school suspensions. But then these other rules did not apply. Kids were not caught in the same situation that was happening at Dudley High School when we first addressed the problem. Okay. So, you know, Dr. Adams and I found that the only way that we could get changes, you know, is that it came a question not of right and wrong, but as the board used to say, we used to have to hold them hostage. In other words, we would cooperate or do what they wanted in order to get them to address an inequity. I think, that was the whole attitude of the board members. Whenever they wanted something done, we'd ask, well, what are you going to do for the black students? We always had to attach something that we wanted, something that we thought was needful, to something that they wanted in order to get them to do it. That was just the way we operated.

KC: Which probably earned you a reputation as a fairly militant school board member as a result?

MK: Well, that was awful strange. Dr. Adams and I laugh about it now. We were often attacked by the newspaper and looked upon as being radical. They used to call me radical. However, you know, we looked upon ourselves as being effective.

KC: Yeah. Well it makes good sense from what you are telling me.

MK: We represented a district, and we addressed the concerns of our district. Our district was extremely pleased with–[bell rings—recorder paused].

KC: Okay. We were talking about the school board. And you were effective getting this done.

MK: We addressed the concerns of our community. We represented two communities. You're talking about other racial problems–the whole election process of the school board is a prime example of racism in Greensboro, particularly. Originally, the school boards; was an appointed position by the city council. There were blacks appointed, but they were not the choosing of the community, they weren't the choice of the community. Filing a suit in a compromise was that the board would be elected. However, the board is elected by the entire city although individuals represent a district. It was a very awkward situation. I think I received 85 percent of our district's support and still lost the election the second go round. And as I said that was 85 percent. In fact, during the primary, I think there were about two thousand votes cast. There were three people running, and I received fifteen hundred of those. So, the choice of a district was unmistakable. The city overrode the choice of a district. What you have now, you have individuals who represent a district but are not answerable to the district. The black community then feels disenfranchised through the whole process because those individuals were not the choice of the black community, nor are they accountable to the black community. They are accountable to the white community because a white community put them in office. We were punished because we were addressing the concerns of the black community. And it was said–you'd have to go through the newspaper articles. I, at one time, got as much ink as President Reagan. But the papers attacked us as not being team players and being radical and all because we saw things from a different perspective. It's interesting that when white folks are vocal and concerned about things, they are concerned citizens. When blacks are concerned and vocal, they're radical. We applaud Jesse Jackson, I mean Jesse

Helms for being effective in the Senate, for addressing the needs of North Carolina. So, we see nothing wrong with him looking or being vocal, addressing the concerns of his constituents. But yet, when Alma and I were being vocal in addressing the concerns of our constituents and had overwhelming support, we as the school board like it had never been attacked before. We also threatened to resign. like I said, in order to get things done, we just had to think of the most unusual ways. We were trying to get them to hire more black teachers, to institute affirmative action. I can't remember, but there were some other issues that we thought were unresolved and the board just refused to address them. It was a very frustrating that being a minority on the board, all you could do was get a second. If the board didn't want to discuss it, they wouldn't discuss it. If the board didn't want to address it, they wouldn't address it. It was just a very frustrating thing that all you could do was, raise it and get a second. That was just as far as you could take it. The only way we could get things done is we had to refuse to cooperate with the board, not give in, or to do some things the board wanted us to do. One of the most effective tools that we discovered was they did not want bad publicity. To get things done, we would threaten to have a press conference, and I had several press conferences. Things just got so awfully bad that the board had agreed to do things and then they refused to do it. We were without a superintendent, and so they just said let's keep harmony. They had promised to do some things and address some things, but they sort of led us until they got a superintendent. Then they just sort of felt, well, we no longer, I mean, we're going to treat you like we were treating you before the superintendent left. We felt betrayed that they were having secret meetings. Just wild crazy things were being done. Dr. Adams and I talked about it, and we said, "well, the board has rendered us ineffective." We had one trump card left, and that was that we could threaten to resign. We felt one of two things would happen. We would either not have the support of the community and we would go on and resign, or the board would be made to see how much support we did have in the community. I guess for maybe a couple of weeks, Greensboro was turned upside down. The chamber was trying to get some corporation here, and when this hit the paper, all that went through. The chamber was jumping up and down. The board of education was trying to get its budget approved by the county commissioner, and the chamber was going against the budget simply because of this. They weren't going to support it. The chamber organized and made some super–committee, and assigned a person to each person of the school board, and told them to get this thing resolved. The chamber asked us not to resign, the human relations asked us not to resign, the school board asked us not to resign, and so all this, you know. But, we did not resign based upon the school board agreeing to do what they said they would do, in instituting an affirmative action because we were discovering that black kids were going through the whole system and some of them had never seen a black teacher, had never been exposed to a black teacher, and had never seen a black teacher at all. It was very possible that, you know, you're not talking about isolated cases. It did, and it does have an effect on blacks when they see that the only person that is in power is white. The only person that they've been exposed to teach them is white; they begin to think then that they themselves are inferior. You're seeing the repercussions of all of this.

KC: I've talked to a number of people who have grown up in Greensboro back in the 1930's and forties and went to Dudley when it was a segregated black facility. Their experience being educated through the system is quite different. They tend to recall it as a time when respect for individuals and achievement and making the most of what one had were very important values that were instilled. You seem to be saying that by the 1980's that situation had pretty well become a thing of the past.
MK: Well, what I think the white populace failed to realize is when you destroy a culture, you also deteriorate respect of

those attributes and qualities that are desirable. The first thing was that Dr. King in the sixties movement was not for desegregation. That was actually a white term, and that was a compromise. They really wanted integration.

KC: Yes, there is a difference.

MK: Difference, you know. You integrate the various cultures. Actually, the United States was made worse because they could have been enriched by the various cultures, you see? You know, if they had been exposed to the various cultures, then actually our system would have been enriched, instead of just one culture dominating the whole system to demolish all other cultures; and that's what took place. The moralities; the morality are not what they used to be. A prime example of this was a lady who ran through the park who was raped by these twenty blacks.

KC: Oh, up in New York?

MK: Yeah, up in New York. What actually took place was it destroyed the cohesiveness of the black community. The black community has just never been the same after desegregation. It destroyed the home. It destroyed relationships and all those things. It was the worst thing that ever happened to blacks. When we had the segregated schools, blacks had a tendency to learn more even though they did not have equal facilities. But what you had, you had teachers who came from their community who were accountable to the community because they attended the same church, ate at the same restaurant, and were a part of the community itself.

KC: Sometimes lived down the block a ways.

MK: Down the block. They knew your mama by name; they grew up with your aunt, and so on, and so forth. You had these ties, and when you have these type ties, you know, the teachers had more liberties to teach and to go the extra mile. When you have this type of tie-in and accountability, you're going to find that the students are just going to do better. It's just no other way, they're going to do better. It was nothing, but you just didn't sass a teacher because the teacher would call your mama. More so, she could hit you and nothing would be said. Nothing would be said at all. It was just different. The teacher would say–it wasn't a question of whether or not you want to do your homework, you will do your homework. You had those factors that are missing now. Blacks are just not doing as well. There are cultural differences that people won't take note of. The board used to say that, the administrations used to say that when they went into the classroom, they didn't see any color. That is the most racist statement to make because being a historian; you know that history plays a part in anybody's background. When you have individuals who are not as richly exposed to things, then it takes more to educate them. I mean, that's what it requires. You find very few blacks that have computers in their home. With their white counterparts, they're brought up with computers. It's gonna require more to orient that, the blacks on computers. It simply has to do with exposure. The whole testing is biased; the whole testing process is biased. And they know it's biased. They know it's biased, but the system refuses to do anything about it. This is just national problem. If blacks were tested on the things that they are familiar with, then they would do better. If we took you out of your natural culture and put you in another culture, then you would reflect it.. It would be reflected that you are retarded or something because you just don't know. These are the type things that we constantly tried to make the system aware of. We instituted some things in the system, and the gifted and talented program has become a model for the whole country. That was because of efforts that were brought in by Asa Hilliard, and he showed some things they were doing that kept blacks out of the gifted and talented program. They broadened the gifted and talented program and found out, indeed, that blacks were and could meet a standard. So it's just–I guess the whole of Greensboro is, and North Carolina, is that there is a very subtle racism. In fact, North Carolina and Greensboro, particularly, and in my opinion, one of the most racist places in this nation. However, it is so subtle until you can't document it, you can't take it to court, and it's nothing tangible. But things are put into the system that brings about the desired results.

KC: Yeah, you can see that particularly in the response to the Brown v. Board of Education in '54. Greensboro was one of the first cities in the Southeast to say "we will comply," and one of the last cities in the Southeast actually to desegregate, under strict court order.

MK: And, when they did it. The other thing I had Dr. Adams to call me. She's supposed to testify in Raleigh, and they wanted to talk about desegregation and integration and what the problems seemed to be. I think one of the most overlooked problems was simply this: I think a fellow named Bull Connor; I guess it was, was siccing the dogs on the blacks.

KC: Mississippi?

MK: Yes. When you took systems to court, and they were ordered by the courts to desegregate, people with Bull Connor's mentality was the ones who desegregated the schools. They were the ones who were in office. You had people who were in power who didn't want to do it and were made to do it. That's why you have what you have. You make people do what they don't want to do, and then quite naturally it's not going to be successful.

KC: Absolutely.

MK: I think that was one of the things that was just overlooked. When the court ordered to do it, who was supposed to do it? They had the wrong people doing it. What

31

you have nationwide is just a grand mess.

KC: Could they have done it differently? If you were given the order in structuring our integration of educational facilities, how could it have been done differently in order to achieve integration as opposed to desegregation?

MK: Well, I think number one, I'm not sure whether or not integration could have ever been achieved because it was requiring–you can't legislate morality. You just can't do it, and you can't make people do what they don't want to do. You can't pass a law that says that everyone's going to get along with each other and love each other. I mean, you just, it's just, it sounds good, but it just doesn't work. I don't know that integration could have been achieved. However, we will never know because it was never tried. What we have, they never tried to integrate the schools. I, we, strengthen the entire chain. Therefore, I think the monies and the resources need to go to the students who need it the most. Okay. That would not be to neglect the GT program, or gifted and talented students. I think we still enhance that. However, it's still I don't want to go. If they can't go where they want to go, they cannot go where they don't want to go. So, you have that. I think we should to deal with reality and community schools if they're structured right. I don't see any problem at all with it. I think the magnet programs can enhance some form of desegregation. I think you can get the magnets to do that. I think more importantly that who sits, whether a black and white sits in the same classroom, is that the blacks and whites are meeting their full potential. I think that should be the question of the day. Are we where they are providing for every student in the atmosphere that that individual can be the very best student it can be? If we can answer that yes, then I think everybody's satisfied. I think now, you know, that blacks and whites are going to go to schools together, naturally those persons who are not racist will have no problems with who their daughters and sons go to school with now. Those who do have problem with it, there's nothing you can do. You just can't make them change. They move out in the county, and the county became predominantly all white in situations. Now they're talking about merging the system again, so they're going to find another way if you try to force them to do it. I don't think that's the challenge of education. I think that we should provide every student the resources to reach their full potential. I think secondarily, if we can do some things that will strengthen and better race relationships, that's time. I don't think it should be a paramount responsibility of education. I think that's sort of what, what happened in the sixties. We were more concerned with numbers in ratios than we were about students and whether or not we're providing the best education we could. We think we need to strengthen the weak links. I think it needs to be done this way. There are throughout this nation situations similar to ours. The worst scenario is someone has been successful in resolving the problems somewhere in this nation. A prime example is the movie they just had out, Lean On Me. This is a man who turns this high school around. What I think we find, we identify what our problems are, then we find someone who has a proven record. The unique thing about Greensboro, Guilford County, is people don't mind spending money on education.

KC: That is very unique.

MK: There are a lot of systems who have problems, but then they don't have any money. What I'm saying is we go locate individuals, specialists in certain areas, and bring them down and ask them how long will it take for you to turn this situation around? Monitor their success, give them a certain length of time, and provide rewards if they're achieved. There's just no problem in our system that can't be turned around. I feel that that would be the most appropriate way of making this system something that all of us can be proud of.

KC: It sounds to me as though you're suggesting possibly a

return to neighborhood schools, then?

MK: Yes, to an extent. Basically, we have that now, anyway.

KC: True.

MK: That was one thing we wrestled with at Dudley. The black population of Dudley decreased every year because the people were getting transferred out. They weren't earmarked to go to Dudley, but there were so many ways to get out of Dudley. So the point, you know, I think that's just a losing, losing struggle. I think we can, we can better utilize our energies in other areas. I think it's just an acknowledgment now that people are going to community schools anyway, or basically going to where they want to go, or least they're able to not go

KC: How about the issue of race relations then? If it's not appropriate that the schools become a focus for that, if schools should educate to the best potential, what becomes the mechanism to enhance improved race relations, which have come a long way since the 1950's?

MK: I tell you what; I think educating kids to their full potential automatically improves race relationships. A prime example, I guess I had gotten so into the needs of the black community that I sort of took on tunnel vision, and I did not realize just how effective white teachers could be with black students. I still hold that we, that they at least need to be exposed to some black presence, okay? But this year my son went to General Greene [Elementary School]. He had a white teacher. And she is probably one of the best teachers I have ever seen in my life—black, white, or indifferent. I'm saying, if we concentrate on educating kids and that black teacher are providing the service she should, and then those parents would be appreciative enough, and with the students the relationship automatically is improved. I think the focus needs to be on education, and then I think these other things has a way of sort of settling themselves. You understand? You know, we have tried busing and all that kind of stuff. I think now if we just concentrate on education, and I think basically that's what every parent wants for his child, and the person who achieves that is going to be recognized by that parent, regardless of the color. If I had my way, I'd leave him in Miss Cook's class another year because she was just, she was just excellent.

KC: Have I forgotten to ask you anything that I should be asking you?

MK: No, not that I know of.
KC: Well, I've just about run out of questions, and I really thank you for your time. Let me just cut this off. [End of Interview]

This article was the epitome of the man that I knew as my father. Over time these articles became harder and harder to find, which is why I cherish this one so much. I remember my mom telling me when I was a young boy our church started a video ministry and would drop a tape off to my father every Monday. My father would review the tape to critique himself, and afterward my mother said I wouldn't let anyone take the tape out. She said I would stand in front of the television mimicking every grunt and movement for hours.

But my father LOVED[1] James Benson Dudley High School (rolls eyes). To this day I may attend some events at Dudley just because it makes me feel closer to my dad, but to me Dudley was the rival sports school that a lot of my friends went to. Historically, Dudley High is one of the most prominent black high schools in North Carolina. It was not until this article that I received the backstory of how hard my father fought to ensure the school that he loved was treated fairly and stayed opened! He also got a big kick out of seeing anyone who knew him from his high school days; whether it was calling him "Champ" for winning the State wrestling championship, or stories of him using his executive privilege as SGA president to skip class... and get his friends out of class too. I even found out later on that Jesse Jackson Jr. was my father's campaign manager when he was running for the school board,

---

[1]interview source http://library.uncg.edu/depts/archives/civrights/detail-bio.asp?bio=64

how crazy is that!

I remember one Christmas the only thing I asked my dad for was a PlayStation 2, it was the newest game console at the time. I was making good grades and stayed out of trouble, so I was very much expecting it as my Christmas gift that year. My dad had a way of surprising you with the very same thing you asked for, his creativity was limitless. A few days later we took our annual Christmas family shopping trip, which as a kid, had become one of my favorite family pastimes. And our first stop was always my most desired destination, Toys R Us.

But when we got inside something really strange happen. My father took my hand and walked me over to the regular PlayStation section and began to ask me what games I wanted for Christmas, you talk about heated! In my head, I was saying, "now I know I told my dad I wanted a PlayStation 2." It was all I had talked about for six months leading into Christmas. I had crossed every T and dotted every I, and this guy has me in the PlayStation section. But two things kept me from losing my head. First, I have always had a humble spirit about myself and even if I was forced to play my PlayStation for another year I was going to be grateful. And secondly, if I had any other reaction outside of my first one my father would have laid me smooth out on that Toys R Us floor (laugh out loud). Plus I started thinking my birthday was only a few weeks away and, all I was going to do was start asking for the PlayStation 2 for my birthday present. At a young age, I found out how to be just as creative in my own youthful way.

So, reluctantly, I picked out some games, and we continued with the night. My father could not but help notice my disappointment following the rest of the night and got a kick out of it. He asked me what was wrong, and I told him that I was fine and then he gave me a lecture on being grateful. I was very much so, but I really wanted my PlayStation2 as well. After dinner, we headed home and unpacked the car. This trip was always done a few weeks prior to Christmas, so there would be a waiting period until we actually got to open our gifts. It was the longest two weeks of a young brother's life, counting down the days until Christmas was a ritual for me.

As a rule, on the night of Christmas Eve we were always allowed to open one gift, but for some reason, my father was making me stay in my room. Our house was always filled with people during this time and everyone was downstairs opening gifts and eating food, and I was subjected to my room. I was pacing back and forth in my room super confused, contemplating about every bad thing I had ever done in life because this was obviously my karma. My father would come open the door to check on me. In my head, I am already in trouble for something that I am unaware of so the best thing to do is keep a cool head to avoid compounded this with a whopping. But after a quick check, he would close the door and tell me to stay there.

After a few moments pass by, I hear my father yelled my name to come downstairs and I nervously move towards the door. Walking down the steps, I took a few sighs of relief because I knew I was not in trouble. But I still could not figure out why I was told to stay in my room away from everyone for so long. As I walked into the family room where my father was, there I saw a brand new PlayStation 2 already set up with Eddie George on the screen who was the featured player on the Madden video game that year. My happiness could not be described in words, I was beyond myself, and my father knew that he got me good.

A few days later we went to church on Sunday as we did most of every Sunday, but at least this Sunday was Christmas Sunday, which meant more gifts and treats. We also got a chance to exchange stories of what we got for Christmas with our friends. So, after Sunday school a few of the friends I had in the church gathered around to share our stories, and then something really strange happened. One of my friends, who were beyond himself describing his gifts, as I was about my Play Station 2, started talking about his brand new Play Station and all the games that came with it.

And as I listened to him talk, I started to notice that he

was calling out all the games that I picked out that night with my Father at Toys R Us. I was floored in that moment, and even at a young age I had recognized what my Father had done for my friend and how happy he was even if he didn't know how it had happened. I found my father after the service and gave him the biggest hug He probably didn't know what it was for because I didn't tell him what I had put together, but the hug was just for him being him.

I have stories like that for days about my father coming to someone's need, and his favorite line was "People need you when they need you; not the day before, not the day after." That was my Father, he had the heart of gold and really loved feeling like he was making the world a better place. But for all of that love and Joy that he had, he still had a large part of Raymond in him, and a temper that could set a wet cloth on fire. I remember my mom telling me this story of a guy coming to my dad and asking him for some money. She said she was pregnant with me and money was tight, but of course, my dad was always a sucker for a person with a problem and a story. He always wanted to seek the best out of a person.

Well, my mom tells me that a few weeks go by and my father does not hear anything back from the guy, these weeks soon turned into months. Well as the story goes, my father was downtown at the courthouse on the behalf of someone else, which is funny in itself because to not have a law degree my father was forever at the courthouse trying to get someone out of trouble. This particular day my father runs into the guy that he gave the money to, and without reacting my father takes off his belt and starts beating the guy in court. Now Mr. Preacher man does not get arrested or anything and proceeds to go home to tell my mom what happen. She says she asked him did he at least get his money back and he replied, "No, but I got about $1,500 worth of a** whooping out of him though" (laugh out loud)

Chapter three: Me against the World

Be grateful for blessings
Don't ever change, keep your essence
The power is in the people and politics we address
Always do your best, don't let the pressure make you panic
And when you get stranded
And things don't go the way you planned it
Dreamin' of riches, in a position of makin' a difference
Politicians are hypocrites, they don't wanna listen
If I'm insane, it's the fame made a brother change
It wasn't anything like the game; It's just me against the world

-Tupac (Me Against the World)

I had a conversation with my brother that ultimately changed the way I viewed my existence. For the majority of my young life, I didn't feel as if there was anything special about me or my birth. By the time I was able to understand what was going on around me, my little sister was born and she took the cake! My sister was the youngest and the only girl in a family of men, on my father's side at least. So, this ultimately put me into the common middle child syndrome. I was much more like my mom in personality (i.e. quiet and to myself)-the true epitome of an introvert who just happens to have extroverted traits. When I think about it, this was probably due to my father always being in the public eye. I knew how to handle myself and my mom did a great job with teaching us how to be well spoken. Until this day, she stills corrects my subject-verb agreements.

I was a big momma's boy growing up. I did not pay my dad any attention until I was about 3 or 4 years old. He was cool, but he wasn't my mom. My mom understood me, she allowed me to be myself with the unspoken understanding that I was her mini-me. My dad thought she was raising me to be soft. I didn't take on the aggressive personality most of the men in my family had, but I never really felt the need to either. I can count on one hand how many times I got a whooping growing up. Do not get me wrong, I did slip up a few times though; pretty bad too. Once I had a childhood friend named CJ and we use to sneak and go to this pool at this apartment complex after church on Sundays. I would ask my parents to go to CJ house and they would usually agree. I would stay until late in the evening.

One particular Sunday CJ suggested that we go to the pool, and I was down because I loved to swim–it was one of my favorite hobbies and still is, but we had walked probably about 3 miles down to the apartment complex, have a good time and walk back. I was probably about 7 or 8 years old. Ironically, I had a pool at my house so it would have just made more sense in hindsight to just invite CJ over to my house to go swimming. Remember, I already said I had a few slip-ups growing up.

At any rate, one particular Sunday my father invited CJ's family to go swimming at our house after church, and as usual, I asked to go over CJ's house with the intentions of going back to the apartment complex. Well CJ and I went to the pool right after church and had a good time. We were about to start walking back to his house. Little did I know my parents had come to pick CJ and me up from CJ's house a little while after we left for the apartment pool. Of course, they began to panic when they found out that I was not at the house and no one really knew where we were.

Lo-and-behold, as soon as CJ and I began to start walking back to his house, my mom and dad drove down the street and we made eye contact. It was the worst eye contact ever. They pulled into the parking lot and needless to say, I began to panic. I knew I was wrong, so the first thing I could think to do was run. I ran about 5 or 6 steps and then stopped. Oh man! That made my dad hit the roof! I turned around and walked to him and proceeded to get the slap of the century sending me to the ground. I guess it goes without saying I got a spanking that night as well.

Another time in my 3rd grade class with Mrs. Anderson, I was taking a spelling test and had a little scheme to remember; the few words I could remember. Now in my defense, I did not cheat for the entire test; there were just a few items that I was not totally sure about. Nevertheless, the teacher caught me cheating, or so she thought. I could tell that she had it out for me and I wasn't one of her favorite students. She was excited to get me caught up in some mess. Later that night, I went ahead and told my parents about what had happened. I worked hard to plead my innocence. My downfall was that I was already making bad grades in Mrs. Anderson class, and our report cards just happen to be coming out the next week. That next week when the report cards came out, everything came tumbling down. Mrs. Anderson called my house! When I got home, I walked into our basement room and saw my dad talking to Mrs. Anderson on the phone. I just froze in my tracks. Needless to say, I got a whooping that night as well.

Overall, those are the two of the few times that I got into trouble. I was a pretty good kid, made good grades, and was decent at basketball; but I always flew under the radar. So much so that one morning my mother woke up and got my sister Bethany ready for daycare and they left the house. My brother Malachi woke up and got ready to go work his summer job with my dad and he left the house. When my father woke up that morning and got his things together, not only did he leave, but he also set the alarm for the house. When I woke up, I was not too concerned but I was wondering why the house seemed so quiet? I mean it was straight silence. I got out of the bed and headed downstairs to get something to eat. I think that I was about 7 or 8 years old at the time. By the time I got to the third step, I had set off the alarm, and the sound was boomeranging around the entire house. I immediately headed for the door with no shoes on my feet and ran smooth across our gravel driveway. I didn't stop until I reached my neighbor's Lane house.

With rocks stuck in my foot, I was struggling to catch my breath and explain to Lane's mother what was going on. She helped me get in contact with my parents so they could clear up the situation. A police officer was called out to the house, and I had to explain to the officer how I was forgotten at the house by everybody. Needless to say, I got to pick out what was for dinner that night.

I knew how to be social enough to hang with the cool kids at school. For as long as I can remember, I had a crew of best friends: Bobby, Mezie, and Jay Wright. My boy Anthony was one of my best friends too, but he moved to another school after middle school. We managed to stay tight though. I really do believe you are who you hang around. Thank God I was blessed to have such a great group of friends. We all came from good homes, and our parents did not take any foolishness. Mezie was the hoop star. Bobby was the funny guy, and Jay Wright was the all-around good guy. Many movies come to mind when I think about our friendship: The Best Man, The Wood, The Brothers–that was us; brothers from another mother.

Things were pretty normal for me for the first 14 years of my life. And that was normal as I knew it. I understood that I was privileged at a young age just by the fact that my house was bigger than a lot of my friends, but I didn't really feel out of place because as a family, we shared everything we had. I still remember the days that I could not wait to get home to play my PlayStation, just to get home and find my room filled with kids from the church already playing. My dad always loved having people over to the house, having cookouts, or celebrating holidays. My childhood was filled with having extended family around me. Constantly having family around me taught me how to share, and I respected my dad always for being as generous as he was. Ultimately people thought he stole money from his business. I didn't bother answering "those" types of questions because I was a child but if it was true, I saw it as him being Robin Hood– providing the poor with life experiences they would have never had without him.

my brother Malachi and I

Childhood friend Joy in Tennessee

I remember times when I would be with my dad and we would be at the church long after the service was finished. People with all kinds of life issues sought out my dad for his advice. As a child, the only thing I could understand is how long it would take for us to get home. In hindsight, I understand now. My dad was very selfless in a lot of ways. He gave so much of himself to other people. Even when I felt as if people did not deserve that much of his time, he would extend his time to them at the sacrifice of what we might have had going on. When I take a look back over my life and I see all the things my father did, I really appreciate who he really was.

I remember as a young child going and sitting in on meetings at attorney Steve Bowden office late on Sunday nights. I had no clue that I was sitting in on the Political Action Committee meetings with some of the biggest movers and shakers of our city. I just sat in the corner without speaking a word, and I just looked around waiting for the special words from my dad signaling that it was time to go. He would say, "Ready to go home, Yellow Boy?" No words sounded sweeter at that time.

I sat at the realm of power at a young age. Whether it was taking photo ops with Governor Jim Hunt, sitting in the living room with Johnnetta B. Cole, or having Oprah's mother stay at our house. Powerful people were the norm for me; they were just people. I didn't really understand the importance they had to society because I was so young, but I always understood the respect they had for my father. People like Alma Adams, Carol Coleman, and Elaine Parmon were all my aunties, not political powers. They were the women who I could go and get a hug from and maybe a dollar for a soda or some candy. I wasn't a part of the master mind think tank, but this exposure was the norm as it relates to the power circle I was engaging with. Further, people like the Rev. Cardes Brown, who is the pastor of New Light Baptist church, was always just "Uncle Cardess" to me. He wasn't the powerful

NAACP leader or a front runner of one of the most prominent churches in Greensboro. He was just Uncle Cardess, or even Dr. Alton Thompson who was a Dean at NC A&T and later became the provost of the school and inducted into the Agriculture Hall of Fame; I didn't know any of that. To me, he was just Deacon Doc, and he was always around. I never knew what the "Doc" represented? I just called him "Doc."

I remember my father doing the Underground Railroad to the polls in which he organized the community under the radar of the media to help Mayor Carol Allen win her mayoral election. It gave my father unprecedented political clot within the city. To this day, many politicians refer to the "Underground Railroad to the Polls" as a successful blueprint of engaging the community in voting. My only gripe about the matter was the fact that I had to wait for him to finish all that he had to do so I could go home. Many times I had to search for a ride to get back to the house because when my father was in a zone, he had no sense of time.

I remember the time we met Tipper Gore, it was around the election time of 2000 and they were campaigning hard in North Carolina. At this point, my dad was a political force who had all candidates in his good graces, and they loved to have him in their corner. My father and a few other pastors put together a political rally at a church which excited me because I was able to leave school early that day. I saw my dad network his way through the event in the realms of people who had a large social status and he did it in a beautiful manner. My siblings and I joke about how bad my father was with names and he would always cover it up by enthusiastically saying "Hey my friend." He immediately made the person feel as if they were on a personal name-to-name basis with him. Kind of ironic right?

The Tipper Gore event happened during that afternoon and later that same evening they held another event at Mount Zion Baptist Church. While the political and religious leaders mingled in the back, my sister Beth and I were trying to get to the snacks. I would say that was the positive about hanging around my dad–people were always offering us food. While over by the table of food, Governor Jim Hunt walked in the room and came to speak to my mother. My dad was somewhere else at the time and as Governor Hunt spoke to her; he turned around and spoke to Beth and me. At that moment a camera guy took a picture of Governor Hunt leaning over to greet Beth and myself; it ended up in the News and Record the next day. Later that week when I went to the barber shop, they had the picture posted on the wall, but again, I was just trying to get some food.

I remember the night Oprah's mother stayed at our house. I remember cleaning the house from top to bottom and getting ready for her arrival. I knew who Oprah was and to a certain extent, I understood why we were doing it. At the time Oprah's mom, in my humble opinion, was not as important as my Nintendo 64 and that's what her coming to the house was keeping me from. So, in my young age, I really didn't care for her too much; but she was a really nice lady. That was the norm though for my father–he always had house guest come to stay with us. Political friends, public figures friends, or some of his pastor friends. My father was the ultimate entertainer and very few people came to stay with us and wouldn't leave without doing whatever my dad was looking for them to do for him.

My dad was a lot of fun… he really was. When he was not being Rev. King or President of Project Homestead, he was one of the funniest and genuine people I or a lot of other people have ever met. And boy could he cook! I loved to eat my dad's ribs or anything seafood related he decided to make. From his stint at running my grandfather's meat and seafood shop, my dad learned to make some meals that were finger licking good. My dad was the best cook ever. My dad tried to make as many of my basketball games as he could when I was growing up. Sometimes that meant him only being able to make one per season. It didn't matter to me though; I never held it against him. I just remember the games he did come to gave me extra incentive to play harder. I love my mother, but I always wanted to please my father.

We went on a lot of family trips, or rather he was going to preach somewhere else or just taking us on family vacations. He was always telling jokes or trying to buy something. I remember going on vacation with Attorney Joe Williams and his wife to the beach. To my understanding, Attorney Williams invited us to go to the beach, so he wanted to treat us well while we were there. I remember at each meal my dad giving me his card for me to go sneak and pay for the bill. I guess you can't get much passed a lawyer though because I would go to the register and the meal would already be paid for.

I remember going to San Francisco so my father could receive an award with Joe Dudley, founder of Dudley Products. What stands out the most about that trip was how humbled my dad was about receiving that particular award. At that point in his career receiving awards was not out of the norm for my father. He had an office full of them, but this particular award he felt as if he did not do as much as the others had done for society. The crazy part about the matter was that this was the same guy who taught me that no matter how big the moment, no matter how excited you are; always act as if you have been there before. For the first time, I saw my father taken back by the moment.

I remember the morning I woke up and my dad was walking around the house waiting to talk on the Tom Joyner Morning Show about one of his first building blitzes. He also did a wedding on the Tom Joyner cruise that I am sure I could get Mr. Joyner to remember if I were to ever run into him. I even had a huge picture of my dad and President George W. Bush when he came to Winston-Salem. The funny thing about the picture is that President Bush is leaning over on my father as if they had been friends for years. Nothing came as a surprise to me after a while about who may have known my father.

There was one particular time I can remember my dad caught an egg on his face. He threw a fundraiser for Project

Homestead at the Koury Convention Center and brought Dick Gregory as the keynote speaker. I do not understand why he thought this was ok? Even in my newly found understanding of whom Dick Gregory is (and I highly respect and revere him), he was certainly the wrong person for this particular event. This fundraiser had city officials, bank executives, and a host of influential figures who happen to be white. If you know how Dick Gregory speaks, you can imagine how bad it got. And trust me, it got really bad.

Dick Gregory was telling all kind of racially toned jokes that no one in the room felt comfortable laughing at… no one but Michael King. On the ride back home my mother tried to tell him what just happened was really bad. He tried to downplay it and said that she was "overreacting," but the next day at the office his phone rang off the hook with upset partners who paid for those tables at the event. They were pissed off at having to endure a full Dick Gregory performance.

That's one thing that I have always appreciated about my mother; she always made sure that I and my sister understood how to interact with other races; whites in particular. She always taught us the principle of being able to go to the white house and talk to the president and then go outside and talk Ray-Ray on the corner and be able to effectively relate to them both. My mommy was my girl… I could be around her all day. But some of the lessons she taught us, I see now was some of the things my dad should have listened too.

My brother told me it took awhile for my dad to play down that Dick Gregory event. He actually said it wasn't until he brokered the deal with Krispy Kreme and got Maya Angelou to cut the ribbon that he forgot about the mishap of that event. I remember going to Virginia Beach as my dad got training on how to run Krispy Kreme. I did not really understanding what was going, on but getting to hang out with the CEO from Krispy Kreme at the time was pretty cool. I knew he was putting one in his new shopping center the Dudley-Lee building, but I had no idea that meant he would be bringing so many donuts home at night. I had eaten so many donuts then that now, I don't even like donuts like that; go figure.

At times I laugh at myself because my perspective was so innocent at the time. I really didn't understand the importance of what my father was doing. I just knew he was doing it, and more than likely he wouldn't be home before I went to bed. I remember before I went to sleep I would go downstairs and call him at his office and he would answer the phone, "Homestead." I would just say "goodnight daddy, I love you" and I could tell that meant something to him no matter how big of a deal he was handling.

My dad had also built his church membership to be over 500 plus. With a beautiful church off of English Street in Greensboro, my father made that church a home and the choir we had was one of the best choirs I have ever heard. Now what I did not understand about my father professionally, I understood completely when it came to church. My father had become one of the most sought after preachers in the nation. I recall many trips to other churches who invited my dad to come speak... so much so that I recognized my dad had two favorite sermons that he would take with him on the road, i.e., "Making it on Broken Pieces," and "Shaking the Snake Off." I think he got a kick out of knowing that I had grown to figure that out. He might have thought I was soft, but he knew I was smart.

I remember the things I cherish the most about our relationships. For some reason, my dad would always take my hand and squeeze it. I would squeeze back and he would respond by saying "why are you starting stuff?" We would go back and forth for hours. I remember one conversation we had I asked him what the afterlife was like. He told me it was like when you are sleep and you have a dream—that feeling but so much better. I remember that conversation a lot when dealing with people passing away. There wasn't anything Michael King wouldn't do for his children. We had an awesome father, and we knew that. He was by no means perfect, but he was the greatest earthly father I could ask for.

Now, when I look back at the year of 2003 that was the tipping point of my life. That March my father was honored by Bennett College who had given him an honorary doctorate degree. This was one of the few things that my father wanted that he did not receive, which was a formal education. Everything about that weekend was so eerie. It was supposed to be the grandest of celebrations for my father... I remember his office being so busy that week in preparation for the event which was that Sunday after church. I remember my brother and me going to GQ fashions that Saturday Night and picking out brand new suits for the next day because we knew it was such a big day for our dad.

The next day there seemed to be a gloomy overcast that would not go away. We went to church that morning as planned and they had our family walk into the church, and we were greeted by a standing ovation and service went on as usual. But before we ended the service, Nate Hargett who is like a big brother to me walked into the church and informed my dad that his father had just passed. Nate's family owns a successful family owned funeral home in Greensboro, and his father was very well-known within the city. That immediately took the wind out of us and our attention had now turned to being there for Nate and his mother.

We gathered in the back and then headed to Bennett College for the formal ceremony for my father. Again, I couldn't help but feel this weird feeling in my stomach that wouldn't allow me to enjoy the day as much as I should have been able to. Once we arrived it was literally the "Who's Who" of Greensboro in attendance... or at least those who liked my father. Dr. Cole was always so gracious towards our family and absolutely adored my little sister. May I remind you once again the only thing on me and Beth's minds was the food!

My dad had a beautiful service for his degree and gave some thoughtful words that I wish I could remember; I just remember the people's reaction to them. Afterward, the reception had all sorts of influential people in attendance to celebrate my father. To a certain extent, I felt guilty because I felt so sorry for Nate. At that moment I couldn't imagine losing one of my parents, but it wouldn't be long that I would be in the same boat.

Later that month, my father had a heart attack after he finished preaching one Sunday and had to be rushed to the hospital. Right after that, our year began to take a turn for the worst–rather quickly. On July 4th while we were at our lake house enjoying the day, our fish tank at home had caught on fire and our house burnt down leaving us to live out of our lake house for the remainder of the summer. Shortly afterward, we moved into an apartment until our house was cleaned and fixed up which took some time.

My father also found out that his CFO and close friend had been stealing money from the company, and my father had to fire him. I think my dad was hurt more than anything because he had fired people before in the past, but I could see how upset he was about having to go through with it. The guy had been a close friend and his wife and my mom was close... even to the extent that if anything had happened to my parents that he would take us on as our legal guardians.

I could see a change in my father's demeanor. He was always so serious at this point. I could tell he was confused at how he should play his cards moving forward. He ended up playing his cards wrong by blocking the guy he fired from another employment opportunity. It is my belief that this was the straw that broke the camel's back because, at that point, the guy knew enough about my dad and Project Homestead that he was able to convince the newspapers to attack my father's characters. Shortly afterward, the newspaper articles started to come.

At first, it was nothing out of the norm to see my dad on the front of the paper. Good, bad, or indifferent, my dad had been on both sides of the fence. This time; however, the newspaper articles had a different tone to them. Before I could even understand what embezzlement meant, I knew it was not good and the way people were acting around us, I could tell they didn't think it was good either. After the first newspaper article came out, I remember my dad going down to the city council steaming mad. I mean this was is the same city "bunch" that had just a few years prior asked him to come in and save another low-income housing organization that had fallen on hard times. My father felt as if he deserved better treatment than what he was receiving.

This is as much as I can speak about this particular subject because I was a child who did not understand the inner workings of Project Homestead. To the best of my knowledge, I still would not have been able to answer not one question about what was going on. I will say that the articles became more frequent. At the same time, things at his church had taken a turn for the worst as well. Some of the members of the church accused my dad of pressuring them sexually. Worst of all, they were men. This hit him the hardest. The front page of the newspaper read: "Rev. King caught up in gay sex allegations."

I remember the day he found out that it was about to be printed in the paper the next day. We were finishing with Sunday service and he called me back to the office with a few of his deacons standing around. He tried his best to explain it, but I could tell he couldn't find the right words. I didn't force him to... I just hugged him and told him everything would be okay. At the end of the day, despite what people thought about my father, he was my dad. He was the man I lived with for 14 years of my life and the person who raised me, so no allegations made against him could affect that. I could tell that it did take an effect on how others began to treat him. That October my father tried to commit kill himself but was unsuccessful. He had recorded formal goodbyes that he felt we should have listened to when they found his body... it was a lot. The church asked him to stop preaching for a while and he even had a falling out with the chairman of the deacon board, but I guess nobody knew about that.

Things came to a head one day when my mom, sister, and I were riding in the car, my dad called the car phone and he just sounded very strange. He started telling my mom about insurance policies and bonds and just kept telling my sister and me how much he loved us. The next morning I woke up and noticed that my dad did not come home. I opened the door to my mom's room and asked her where dad was and she just told me that he was with my uncle Ray. I just left it at that and went to school as normal. At this point, I had started my freshman year in high school.

Later that afternoon my mother came to pick me and my sister up from school which was rather odd because she was usually at work while we were at school. She drove us over to the Project Homestead's office and once we pulled up, she told my sister to go inside. Once my sister left the car, my mom told me that my dad had attempted to commit suicide the night before. She also told me that she was going to ask for a divorce. All of a sudden I felt my innocence seep out of my being, and I realized that things wouldn't be going back to normal just as I had hoped.

The bazaar fact of the matter was that the weekend prior, my father had taken my sister and me to radio shack, and I saw him purchase a voice recorder and some blank tapes. For the remainder of the day, I just remember him in a room talking to the recorder. The next day my father decided to go spend some time in Knoxville. Once I got back to Greensboro, the first thing I did was went to the car and listen to all the tapes he had recorded. He recorded about ten of them, and I listen to them all. He had ones for the church, for homestead, for my mom, for Malachi, his secretary, and for beth and I.

When he came back to Greensboro, he went to go stay at the lake house and I could tell that he was not himself anymore. Truth be told, he was already dead. He didn't want to be around people and he didn't want to go anywhere. I remember one day he walked passed me and it wasn't unusual for us to hug and embrace each other for a long time but that particular day, he broke down crying in my arms. I don't know if you know what it feels like to have your

53

Superman crying in your arms but for me, it was an empty feeling. He just kept saying that he hoped that he was a good father and that he only wanted to do right by us. I had never seen my dad so emotionally unstable. Heck, I had only really seen him cry once or twice in my life... but never sobbing as he was... never.

After that moment, I wanted to be around my dad as much as possible. I could see that he was hurting, and there were not too many people in his corner. It was affecting him. I would call him during the week to remind him that I was coming to spend the weekend with him just to keep his spirits up. One day he called me right after I got out of school and asked me if I was coming to see him and I ensured him that I was, but I could tell in his voice he was in a bad place.

Part II: Prince
Chapter Four: December 4th

Now I'm just scratching the surface
'Cause what's buried under there
Was a kid torn apart once his pop disappeared I went to
school got good grades could behave when I wanted
But I had demons deep inside that would raise when
confronted
Hold on

-Jay-z (December 4th)

That Thanksgiving was weird. It was the first time that I could remember that our holiday wasn't filled with people around and that spirits seemed low. It was as if we were going through the motions to make it through the day. My father had not always been the most fashionable person, but those days it seemed as if he really didn't care about his appearance and that was so unlike him. The next week my high school had advanced to the state championship game in football and I really wanted to go to the game.

So, instead of going to the lake house that Friday night as I usually did during that time, I stayed at the apartment so that I could go to the game that Saturday morning with the intentions of going to see my dad afterward. That Thursday evening, I had called my dad to tell him my plans and told him I would see him Saturday. We told each other we loved each other, and that was that. Little did I know that would be the last time I would ever speak to my dad.

Once I got back from the game., which my school lost, I was ready to get to my father. I started to call his cell phone, but he wasn't picking up. I started calling the lake house too, but he wasn't answering that phone either. My mom had to go to work, so she just dropped me off at my God brother Rodney's house since that evening he was being promoted at work and my dad was supposed to be coming with us to that function. Without anyone knowing, I had begun to call my dad every hour on the hour... then every 30 minutes... then back to back... and still no answer. In my spirit, I felt as if something was wrong and when Rodney's mother arrived at the house who I call "DiDi," I told her that I had not talked to my dad all day and that I was worried. Everyone ensured me that he was just probably out on the lake fishing and left his phone in the house which he had a habit of doing. But as the evening grew it became apparent that something was wrong.

Another family friend went out to the lake house to check on him and once he got there, he called back to

Rodney's house. I could tell something was terribly wrong by everyone's tone. Didi told Rodney that they needed to go get my mom from work and head out to the lake house. Didi gave me a hug and told me everything would be alright and she and Rodney left the house. I went into the living room and just sat down in a daze... wondering what possibly could be so wrong. After falling asleep on the couch, I woke up to hear the garage door opening and a lot of people walked into the house.

My mom walked in behind them, and I could tell something was wrong by how quiet everyone was... in an almost somber mood. My mother walked over to me and whispered: "Your father went to go be with the Lord" and almost immediately, that opened up the floodgates and gave everyone permission to start crying. I just collapsed into Didi's arms; I never cried so hard in my life. Then my mother went upstairs to tell my sister the news. I could tell when she told her because my sister just started screaming. It was such a surreal moment. It was like a bad dream. My mom came back downstairs and asked if they could drop us off back at the apartment. Everyone wanted us to stay, but she insisted that we are dropped off.

At the same time, Jay-Z had dropped the Black Album and a lot of the content of the album dealt with him losing his father. When I got into the, car I just put on my headphones and played his song December 4th. I never thought a song could be so relevant to my life than that moment. I just remember the car being so quiet on the way back and me, just looking up at the sky... it was full of stars. When we got back home, I was heading to my room and then my mom asked me and my sister to sleep in the bed with her that night. She never asked us to do that before and strangely enough, we didn't cry that night or anything... we all just got in the bed and went to sleep.

I was the first one to wake up the next morning, and I remember feeling so numb. I couldn't figure out if what had happened had really happened or if it was just a bad dream that I had not woke up from. When I went to my room and sat on my bed and turned on the T.V. the news flashed came up. "Breaking News: Rev. Michael King is dead... Details at 12." and then my phone rang, it was my brother Malachi. He had gotten locked up in jail a few days before and just found out the news. He was a wreck, and it was too much for me to deal with at the moment because at the same time Beth had woke up and was in her room crying and screaming for my father while gripping a picture of him. When I walked to the door, my mom was in there comforting her and I just looked at my mom and said: "Well I guess I'll call Mrs. Hargett." At that moment I had decided I would try to be as strong as I could for my mother because I only could imagine what the next few days would hold.

I called Mrs. Hargett, and she had already heard the news. She told me she was proud of how strong I was being but to be honest, I was still numb; I couldn't cry if I wanted to. After we got off the phone, I just sat on my bed and gazed off into space. I understood that my life would never be the same again. Not too long afterward people begin to show up at our apartment. Floods and floods of people came. By nightfall, we had so much food and anything else we could have possibly needed. The support was so notable. A few of my friends came by too. I am still grateful for all of them.

The sad part of the story was that I could tell a lot of those people felt guilty for not being there with my father and a whole a lot of finger pointing started to go on. I could tell the anger was out of hurt. Not only would my life never be the same again, but that was the reality for a lot of other people; our lives would never be the same again. I think the hardest part of that week was the fact that I couldn't escape it. Of course, it was on the front page of the news the next day.

The first story on the news... even when I got in the car, the radio stations were talking about it too. At that point, I was really searching for as much space from people as I could get. My only indifference with people was that: "where was all this concern when my dad was alive? Why now? Why did they want to help? All of a sudden you want to help now?" By this time, it was too late, he was gone.

We had a memorial service and a funeral service for him that week. Being in attendance was very hard. All week I was still holding out for the chance of possibly waking up and just realizing it was a bad dream but when I walked into his memorial service and saw his picture. It hit me that he wasn't coming back. I didn't go to his wake.

I didn't want the image of seeing my dad dead in my head. Thankfully my mom did not make me either. I still tried my best to hold myself together for the sake of my sister and my mom. I did really well during the memorial service until I saw my Uncle Billy break down and start crying. He and my dad look JUST alike; it was too much for me. One of my father's close friends and fellow preacher saw me walking outside to the back of the church to be by myself, he stopped me and hugged me. I immediately broke down in his arms and everything I held in during the week just poured out at that moment.

The next day I just remember waking up not wanting to go to the funeral service. I wasn't ready to say goodbye to my dad. I mustered up enough strength to make it to the service and once I finally got to the church, strangely enough, I didn't want to leave. For both services, I had never seen the church so packed. When I walked in the first thing I noticed was my brother was there in handcuffs with two sheriffs standing beside him. I didn't want to be next to the casket, so I sat two rows behind my mom and my sister. But I felt my dad's spirit in the building from the moment we pulled into the parking lot. It was a beautiful service. We sang his favorite gospel songs, laughed, and received an awesome message. I had done well all the way up to the point that they were about to start moving the casket out of the church... I broke down again.

After the service, I went to the back of the church as everyone passed by his body one last time. My mom asked me to go to the burial site with her and I agreed.

Congresswoman Alma Adams   Helena Henry

We held each other's hand as they dedicated my dad's body back to God and I got up and kissed the casket the same way I use to kiss my dad's forehead. I was forced to say goodbye to my Superman. I didn't know how I was going to move forward in life nor did I understand at that moment that my life would totally change. All I knew was that Superman was gone.

Months following, the newspaper articles kept coming, and they only got worse. My father was no longer here to defend himself, and the way he died almost made him automatically guilty in the court of public opinion. To pour salt on the wound, my mother was not really herself anymore and I could see a change in her too. All of a sudden, a new guy had come into her life and would ultimately put a wedge between our relationship. I had no bias against the guy because I didn't know him from Adam—all I knew was that he was taking the attention I was used to getting from my mom. I remember that New Year's Eve was the first time I had spent outside of the church. I wasn't ready to go back just yet, but the guy ended up taking my mom to the beach and that New Year's Eve, I cried like a baby feeling as if everything had gone to hell in a handbasket.

The next few years would be some of the darkest of my life. The guy ended up marrying my mom and moved into our house. Not to dwell too much on this subject, but let's just say he and I didn't see eye-to-eye about almost anything. This ultimately forced me to move out of the house after an episode in which, I myself, was about to commit suicide. I was at a point that I couldn't take my living situation. This guy who married my mom had been engaged to her in college and I guess they reconnected over this time. The crazier thing was the fact that I found out that he knew my dad and that he even allegedly was spotted at my dad's funeral.

I didn't know anything about him and what made the situation more brash was the fact he never sat me down and said: "Hey Matt, my name is such and such, and I am from such and such, my favorite food is such and such, and I met your mom at such and such." Instead, I got an invitation to a bible study to which he sat down and pulled out verses about obedience, as if I didn't know about these verses being the son of a preacher. I didn't appreciate the approach of control at all. Not only that, but he begins to control my mom finances. Funny enough I never saw him get up for a day of work ever while he was living in the house and my mom was working over 50 hours per week. I think that's how she started to cope with everything; she just started to hide at work.

I remember he came down with a red Volvo I didn't think anything was special about it. Months later, after moving into the house there was a black Benz and BMW in the garage, and I never saw my mother drive either one. My issue wasn't with the cars; my issue was that my mom started neglecting me and my sister for his benefit. Even after working hours upon hours and him being home all day, she will still come home to fix him a hot plate of food while telling me and my sister to go make a sandwich. Then he would tell me and my sister that we couldn't use the kitchen, microwave, stove, or the George Foreman grill.

To add insult to injury, he would never tell me to "do

anything" to my face, he would always make my mom do his dirty work. Two deal breakers came when he purchased another German Shepherd. We already had one that my dad had purchased and it was trained. I know that dog cost thousands of dollars and this dog was trained to be very vicious. This man's dog barked at me all the time. Every time I entered the room he would go crazy. I knew he was trained to do that. The second deal breaker was when my mother stopped giving me lunch money. At that point, I knew the writing was on the wall for me. The hardest thing I had to do was to leave and that meant leaving my little sister… but I had too. My emotions were too high, but I Thank God for being a Keeper though. God never took his hands off of me… even in my darkest moments.

Luckily I was able to move in with Didi, and I was still able to continue to go to the same high school. But a different fight would start now. With the articles still coming in calling my dad a crook and gay and the fact that at the start of school everyone is forced to read the newspaper in home room, everyone knew what was going on and that I was Rev. King's son. It got to the point where Mezie would just grab the sports section for me so I wouldn't have to read the newspaper's headline. He knew how hurt I was at the fact that they wouldn't just leave my dad alone; he was dead... and it seemed like they were spitting and dancing on his grave. One day I was standing in the front of the school and a guy came to me and said: "Hey I heard your dad was gay." Almost immediately I had a ghost face. Not knowing what to say, a guy name Antonio Hall, who I love until this day and consider one of my biggest influences, stepped in and made it clear that no one was to ever say anything sideways to me again about my father... and that was that.

Droopy, Antonio Hall & DJ Cuttz

The second worst day of my life outside of my father dying was a day during my junior year when I walked into the home room as usual, but this particular day Mezie passed me the front page. To my surprise, the article stated that no criminal charges would be pressed against my father. I had to leave the class for a moment and go to the bathroom to get myself together. In a strange way, I wanted them to find something that way it didn't seem as if my dad died in vain. I was like "you mean to tell me y'all did all that press writing and you aren't going to file any charges?" I was so hurt. It took me a while to come to peace with that. It was one particular writer whose name I won't mention, but his name was attached to every negative article I read about my father. His name burns the ceiling of my memory.

During this time, I do not know where I would be if it was not for the friends God has placed in my life; especially Antonio. He was two years older than me and stepped in to fulfill the big brother role Malachi left when he was sent to prison. I looked up to him in every way possible. I wanted to be just like him... he was cool. He was a multi-sports star and was attached to a lot of females. But he always took the time to spend with me to keep my head level. His family became my family. I was always with him. He was the first person to teach me how to drive (although I almost killed us–laugh out loud) and I got my style and demeanor from him. If I didn't know how to handle myself in a situation, I would just look at Antonio and mock what he did. His senior year he won Homecoming King and shortly afterward he deemed me "Prince." That's how I got the name if anyone was wondering. And at the time being "Prince" to Antonio's Kingship was better than being known as Rev. King's son; at least to me it was.

Antonio went off to college and set a great example of what I knew I wanted to do. I wanted to go to college. I had a core group of best friends... starting with Jermaine and Anthony. Both of them moved during High School so we weren't as close as we would have been, but when we all got together, it was like we never were apart. I still had my C.O.S crew–Class of Seven or Circle of Success... but Mezie, Bobby, Jay Wright and later my boy Ish, we ran together hard.

I knew Mezie the longest... out of the crew we were the closest. I had known Mezie since kindergarten and we had played on many basketball teams together. I spent a lot of time at his house growing up. My dad uses to clown around with Mezie when we were on the phone together growing up. Our parents approved of our friendship because they knew we both came from good homes. Mezie and I use to prank call people, had the meanest NCAA Football video games battles, and he has always been a stable force in my life.

J Wright, Bobby, Ish, Mezie, Tee & Kee   Jermaine and J Wright

I met Bobby in second grade. We were in the same class and his birthday was a day before mine. He is the friend that I am most like; we have a lot of personality traits that are alike. I guess that's the Capricorn in us; we are laid back. Bobby is also the funniest person I know by far. Jay Wright came into the crew in 8th grade. At first, I thought that he was a nerd. He and Bobby became close friends over time and Bobby kind of brought him in the group. Ultimately, I was always with Mezie. Bobby was always with Jay Wright and we were always together. Jay is one of the most sincere people I have ever met. He is very passionate and has a big heart. He is also the "lover boy" of the group (laugh out loud).

I had known Ish since we were little kids. We played some AAU basketball together and came up together at Hayes-Taylor YMCA. He transferred to our school our senior year and fit into the group perfectly. He and Bobby were clowns. It was never a dull moment with us. Then there was Markee and Tee who were a year younger than us, but we're still family. We become the "cool good guys." We all made good grades and even our principal, Dr. Walker who was a black lady, recognized that we all had bright futures. We all knew we were going to college, and we never got caught up in the foolish stuff most of our peers were getting into at the time. We knew more was expected from us.

I love my friends because they kept my life as normal as

possible. They all knew what I was going through, but we never talked about it and they never asked about it. They just focused on being my friend, being teenagers, and enjoying high school. Ambitious, we all graduated from high school and went to college. I also had two female best friends: Kiara and Tiara. They both were considered two of the most attractive girls in school and because of our interaction people thought I was involved with one or the other. They were just two of the most reliable people I had in my life at that time. They listened to my life problems, I gave them boy advice, and they helped me learn how to attract females. I allow them both to share the credit in the monster I became when I got to college. I love both of them to the moon and back for being there for me when I needed them the most.

I had two teachers who had profound impacts on my development. Ms. Woods and Coach Slade made a huge contribution to my life. I had a slight crush on Ms. Woods, not in a perverted way but I loved the way she carried herself. She ended up being someone I could talk to, someone I could vent too–she always motivated me to do more with my life and encouraged me to be great. My love for her is unwavering.

Coach Slade was my hero! He was the cool young black teacher at the school. People said we favored and even got a look-a-like award in the yearbook one year. Ms. Woods was more hands on and Coach Slade was more indirect. All the girls loved Coach Slade, but he always carried himself with a manner of respect that you knew he was all business. The main thing I knew was I had to go to college if I wanted to be like Coach Slade, and I wanted to be just like him. I thank both of them for their influence on me, and I can honestly say that their interaction with me help set me on my path.

I had always loved playing basketball and although I wasn't the best or the tallest I was a pretty decent player. After my dad passed away, I lost my passion for basketball. I had started playing organized basketball at 8 or 9 years old and had the pleasure of playing AAU basketball and coaching summer camps for Mike Harris with some guys who play in the

NFL or NBA. Still, the best basketball player I ever played with personally was Mezie. Our friends use to joke that he was just 3 inches short of the NBA, but we had played together since Middle school.

I really enjoyed basketball, I had fallen in love with the game at an early age going to the gym and courts with Rodney. When I was young, I use to love to watch his high school basketball games video tapes as a child. Growing up my favorite player hands down was Trajan Langdon. I would go to the gym and shoot and yell "TRAJAN." I followed his game from Duke to Cleveland, and I probably made almost every game he played against Charlotte.

I was really good at remembering players' names and stats, and this was at the age of seven or eight years old. I remember my mom dropping me off at the barber shop and coming back to find the barbers in awe and laughter from my knowledge of the game, and of course my articulate argument on how UNC will always be the lesser of the two programs (laugh out loud). I remember every UNC and Duke game Mezie and I would call each other during commercial breaks to talk junk to each other. That conversation would carry on until the loser didn't answer once the game had been decided. You could bet that whoever won would have the newspaper the next day just in case the other forgot.

Going into highschool I got an opportunity to go to team camp at Lees Mcrae College and play against other high school teams. I was playing on the JV level at the time and Antonio and his friends were on the varsity level, but we all got to practice together. That was an added incentive on getting to go. Antonio hung out with a crew called the "Four," and it was him, Curtis, Jaren, and Ricky. In our eyes, they were the older version of our crew, the cool guys who play sports but are well rounded, and all were hilarious.

I can truly say some of the best times I've had in life were in those dorm rooms that summer soaking up all the pre-high school knowledge I could get. I would have stomach cramps from laughing so hard, especially when Antonio and

Ricky would go at it. Ricky was originally from Queens, N.Y. and you heard it in every joke punch line he said. It was never a dull bus ride with those guys and even at a young age, they all took me under their wing in one way or another.

I use to play for Coach Mike Harris who was a legendary figure in the basketball world of Greensboro. If you played basketball in Greensboro not only did you know Coach Harris, but you looked up to Coach Harris. Around the 9th or 10th grade, he would bring back old players to help run his famous summer youth basketball camps. One summer myself, and childhood friends Josh Chavis and Will Graves were selected to help run the camp. We got paid $100 a week for the camp. Will use to make some funny jokes about our payment schedule. He would say, "They better have my money!"

Will was a funny guy. I guess you could have called him the "Lebron" figure of Greensboro basketball during that time. He and Josh went to Dudley High school, which was considered the basketball powerhouse. They won multiple state titles. I didn't care though. I went to Northeast, and we kind of had a chip on our shoulder in our own right because I really did believe Mezie was underrated in comparison to the top players in the state like Will. I will never forget, the first time I ever saw a naked girl on a phone was on Will's phone. He had a Sprint phone, #memories. Coach Harris passed away my Junior year in college and Greensboro basketball misses him dearly.

After my dad passed, I wasn't the same player. Going into my junior year of high school, we got another coach. Coach Hunter came from A & T and played with Michael Jordan at UNC. He was the smoothest coach in terms of demeanor I have ever played for. Going into the season, 3 of us including myself, still played football.

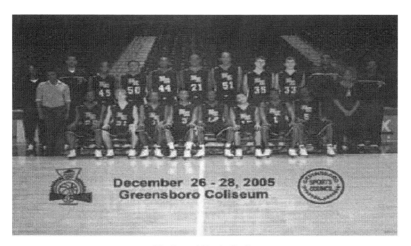

December 26 - 28, 2005
Greensboro Coliseum

Northeast Basketball

So, we didn't join the team until a few games into the season. That year our team was stacked. Not only did two other point guards from other schools transfer in but we also had two other big men transfer in. One of the big men transferred right before the season started. We always said that he would have been the difference maker against Dudley.

We knew we had a good team though. The two guards were my homeboys, Guy and Sam, who I had known and played ball with since childhood. Sam went on to be the starting point guard at the University of Oklahoma. They were both starting point guards at their own school prior to transferring into us, and they both were way better players than I was. I was salty about the fact that I knew my minutes were going to be cut, but I knew the team was better now. I, myself, was still distracted by what had happened with my mom after my dad died.

We started the season out great after losing the opener. We reeled off 8 or 9 wins in a row prior to the big Christmas tournament. Our team was strong and was hoped for a good showing in front of the city. Our first game was against Greensboro Day School which was like the private school powerhouse in Greensboro. My older God brother Rodney was a star guard for them growing up and was close with their

Coach, Coach Johnson. The morning of the tournament we had a shoot-around at the coliseum and we arrived as Greensboro Day was leaving. Coach Johnson and I exchanged a few words. He mentioned it was ashamed Rodney didn't bring me to Greensboro Day.

Later that day during the game I am not sure what happened, but we came out kind of flat. The other team was very good too. It was one of those games where it wasn't a blowout but it wasn't really close either. I think we lost by like 12 or 13 points and Coach Hunter was pissed. After the game, Pizza Hut who sponsored the event, left about 10 boxes of pizza waiting for us in the locker room. So yeah, we were sad, but we were also hungry. A few of us started digging into the pizza as soon as we got into the locker room and that was a bad move.

Coach Hunter walked into the locker room and looked around without saying a word. He walked back out and a few minutes came back in to instruct everyone to get back on the bus. Once we got back to school, he told us to drop our bags and head to the gym which was kind of abnormal considering how late it was and the fact that we had another game scheduled for the next day. We figure he just wanted to run through a few things on the court. We were terribly wrong.

We walked into the gym and the shot clock had been activated, and he told us to get on the line. He then proceeded to run the tongues out of our mouths... and any basketball player will tell you it's a difference between suicides and timed suicides. Timed suicides means if you don't make it before the shot clock goes off it doesn't count. Needless to say, pizza vomit was everywhere, and I was no good. I left the gym, and I was angry.

Looking back at that night, I should have never left. I should have stayed and finished my sprints. At the same time, I was already upset at Coach Hunter because more than anything else, and at the time, I was looking for a father figure, not just somebody to beat me down about basketball. I was having a mental block on the court but I guess he either never put two and two together or didn't bother to. I got back to the house that night and called Rodney and told him what happen and the next week I was at Greensboro Day meeting with Coach Johnson.

We scheduled for me to take a placement test which I did and we also had to file for financial aid, which I did. I scored well on the test and I was brought in for a day visit. I had a guy named Johnny Thomas and Jay Wilson to give me a tour of the school and might I add the school was a very plush. The school offered a quality type of college environment, and if you saw how much it cost, you would understand. I think the biggest thing that stood out to me about this school was walking around the parking lot and seeing kids just jump in and out of expensive ass cars. I remember looking at Jay asking, "Are students allowed to park alongside the teachers?" He laughed and said, "this is the student parking lot, teacher's park on the other side." I looked around to the other parking lot and saw BMW's, Range Rovers, and this beautiful miracle whip color Lexus with rims on it. You name it… Greensboro Day students and teachers were driving it. It was kind of intimidating to say the least, especially coming from my former lifestyle.

Another thing that stood out was the fact that in between classes there would be hallways lined up with chess boards and the thing to do was to get in a quick game of chess between classes. It blew my mind and I couldn't understand the reasoning behind it, but chess is a mental game. This was my first insight on access to quality education or in my case, a lack thereof. I really enjoyed the classes there though they were very laid back and ran a lot more like college classes. This type of environment could only be experienced if I was taking AP classes (Advanced Placement classes) in the public school sector.

All in all, they wanted me to re-class and become a junior again. It took me about two months to decided not to go through with it. It was going into my senior year and all Bobby, J Wright, and Mezie had been talking about were graduating…

together. So instead of going to talk to Coach Hunter and getting back on the team, I did not; pride killed my basketball career. I could go on and on reminiscing about what could have been, but then again, you never know what life has in store for you.

Chapter Five: U Don't Know Me

Contrary to yo beliefs, I'm as real as you can be
F*%k yo thoughts and yo feelings, ni**a you don't know me

-T.I (U don't Know Me)

Derek Blacknall

During the summer of my junior year, I met this guy name, Derek Blacknall. He was a football star at Dudley high school. He was signed to play football at ECU. We hung out a few times, and I got introduced to his twin Cedric. At the time Didi worked third shift, so I was the one in high school with the house to myself. All my friends would come hang out with me. One day Derek was like we should throw a party and make some money.

Cedric and I thought it was a good idea, so we put the plans together to throw a party that summer. I received a social security check each month from my dad so I used that as the money to put in to the party. At the age of 17, I was bitten by the King's entrepreneur bug. At the time it was a social media site called Bebo that was really popular and that's how we decided to promote the party. Derek and I went to the YMCA downtown and booked the gym to throw the first party in. I got the DJ and security together and everything was set. We called it the "Summer Throw Down" and promoted the party for like a month on Bebo... no flyers... no radio ads... just Bebo.

The night of the party I arrived first, and it was already a line waiting for the party to start... I handled more of the business side, Cedric handled more of the social side, and

Derek was the life of the party. I set up the table at the front with an empty money box and had Antonio to help me out. I think we charged 8 dollars for girls and 10 for guys. Within the first thirty minutes, we had a box full of money, and the crowd became bigger than we had ever expected. I had the manager of the YMCA come up to me during the party and offer us the YMCA gym to do parties more often during the upcoming year. We were on to something.

But of course, Murphy's Law was in full effect that night, and anything and everything that could go wrong did. First, a huge brawl started in the party and the security that I hired ended up getting beat up. It started storming outside and after we pushed those who were fighting out, we decided that we had made enough money for the night. It was time to close up shop. Needless to say, the manager at the Y had retracted his offer. Derek and I were satisfied, so we decided to go on and head out of the party. We got two minutes down the road and Cedric calls us to say that someone had started shooting inside of the party. Murphy's Law was on steroids that night!

But at the end of the night, we had made almost $1,200 dollars each and that started me on a totally different path going into my senior year. I was still very involved in school and was the SGA Vice President that year, but all of a sudden the preacher's kid was a highschool party promoter. This was something I KNOW my dad would not have gone for if he was still alive, but he wasn't, and I enjoyed the newfound lifestyle. As Jay-z put it in his song December 4th, "I'm a hustler now... my gear is in and I'm in the in crowd and all the wavy light-skinned girls is loving me now... my self-esteem went through the roof, man, and I got my swag." I never wanted to sell drugs. I never wanted to endanger my future, but throwing parties gave me a legal hustle, and I started to go by Prince all the time. No first name... no last name...just Prince.

My senior year was bittersweet. It was the first year I didn't play school ball which was different considering that I spent my entire school career waiting to play ball as the senior. I enjoyed making money, and unlike all the good basketball players in the city, there were only a few party promoters.

Our next party was a party we should not have even been able to attend ourselves. We were throwing a 20th birthday party at Club Touch which was an 18 and up club and did not cater to high schoolers at all. So Antonio, Cedric and I headed to meet with a guy name Hovair about the details of the party. Nervous because I did not want him to guess my age I went above and beyond in our conversation to ensure him we would have a great crowd.

The night of the party it starts slow, and in comparison to the high school party we threw earlier that summer the night wasn't looking good. One thing that I did not take into consideration was the fact that only at teen parties do people show up on time. About a hour into the party there was people everywhere and the partied had turned out to be a success and I was beyond excited. Unfortunately, we did not do good numbers at the bar and had to split the door with the club and only walked away with a few hundred dollars to split, a far cry from our first party.

While we were in the back counting the money another guy walks into the room and immediately starts counting money. Now I am young but I am not dumb and I had not ever seen this guy before so I am confused at why he was so comfortable touching all the money and why Hovair would let him. After a few moments I hear Hovair say "Yeah Q we still got to pay the security". At the moment I had realized that I was staring at "Q Diddy", who growing up always heard about him and a guy name Z Tweezy throwing parties and doing big things around the city.

So I finally opened my mouth to ask Q what he thought about the night's turnout and he replied it was decent minus the bar not making its money but all things considered a good night. We split the money up and before I left I regretfully stated with confidence " Well I think I can do much better with a little time...plus I am only 17". As my grandma would say you could hear a rat piss on cotton. Q Diddy stared at me for a while and then finally said "that's what's up, give me a second and let me holla at Hovair for a second". I don't what they talked about but by the time I got to IHOP Antonio was pissed at me, he had apparently talked to Hovair before he left and it wasn't a pleasant conversation to say the least. It was a quick lesson in when and who to tell my business to. Q Diddy and I have developed a little mentor and mentee relationship and whenever I am in town he always provides wisdom and sound advice. What up Q!!

A family friend Walter T. Johnson was a teacher at Dudley and had heard about our success. He decided to bring us together as a group and mentor us in the entertainment industry. Walter had thrown concerts, boxing matches, and a host of other entertainment based events. We expanded our circle to include my boy Torrie and C.J. They both attended Dudley as well. Our mode of operation was if they got most of Dudley to come to the party I would take care of the other surrounding schools, and boy was it a successful model. For the majority of our senior year, we were making money throwing high school parties and created a brotherhood amongst ourselves.

After a while, we all had different motives and decided to part ways as a group, but they will always and forever remain my brothers. We all attended and graduated from college. Unfortunately, Derek was killed in December 2013. It was a devastating loss to the city of Greensboro and to all that loved them, especially for his twin Cedric.

I had begun to turn into a little ladies man myself, but it was in the most innocent way possible. I went to 6 proms my senior year escorting all the ladies to their prom and being a gentleman while doing so; however, my frequent appearances did not go unnoticed. After a while, I started calling myself "Pretty Boy Prince." I used it as my party name to go under the radar, but it caught on and as my grandparents would say, I was "smelling myself" a little.

After we parted ways, I continued to throw parties. At this time I was introduced to a DJ in the area name E Sudd and a guy name Ace. He was an upcoming DJ from High

Point and had just come off of DJing on BET's Rap City which was a huge deal. E Sudd let me shadow him, taking me to college parties, and introducing me to my set of mentors. One in particular, was a guy named Miguel Pena or "Swiss" who was attending UNCG at the time. I consider Swiss to be my OG. He was the first person to introduce me to Alpha Phi Alpha Fraternity, Inc. and I thought he was the coolest person ever.

Ace had thrown events around the city, and he and I partnered to throw parties after I left my Dudley group. This was the first time I struck out on my own to throw parties. I was nervous to see if I could pull it off because Ace wasn't in high school, so a lot of the promotion fell on my shoulders. I had to go to the drawing board and figure out how to make this thing work.

One event that helped me build the allure of "Prince" was participating in Delta Sigma Theta's High School Jabberwock Pageant, which had some of the prettiest and most popular girls around the city competing. At the time I had a dear friend of mine FeNe who was a Dudley cheerleader. She asked me to escort her in the pageant, and although she and I were just friends, she had now given me a platform that I was going to take full advantage of. I mean to be a Jabberwock Escort you had to be a "cool dude." This was clout, and I was also lucky enough to be paired up with some of my boys after they were asked to be escorted as well (shout out to the escort crew Bobby, D Best, Kevion, Ced, C.J., Mike.. and the rest of the fellas.. Good Times).

Ace was really plugged into record labels and the radio station. He helped me establish relationships with people like Chris "Sho Smoove" Lea, Waleed Coyote, and Sho'Down Yo baby's daddy. All of them were personalities on 102 Jamz, and they help me leverage what I lost by operating solo against moving in a group.

Delta Jabbawok   Promoting for Ladies night 2

I was able to go to the radio station and promote my parties, and I began to recruit the prettiest girls at each school to help me promote the parties. I would take them with me to the radio station, and of course that would help me increase my popularity amongst the prettiest girls around the city. Ace has this concept of charging ladies a dollar for the party and calling the parties "Ladies Night." I would get somebody from the radio to come host the party and get a local artist who had a song on the radio station to come and perform. I wanted to turn a regular party into more of a concert event. DJ E Sudd would come and rock the party, and all of a sudden I was the go-to-person when it came to high school parties. I made a lot of money, and I started being recruited by the college promoters to come and help them promote parties. They wanted me to go to NC A&T so I could be around, but that would have been like 13th grade for me. I had to get out of Greensboro because no matter who Prince became in Greensboro, I was still Rev. King's son.

Chapter Six: College Boy

Yeah, uh, I hate to brag,
well naw, I don't, the big man on campus
I gotta chick in every class that give a ni**a glances

-J. Cole (College Boy)

Brint City

I remember a conversation I had with Sho Smoove (Chris Lea) one day. I asked him what should I strive to do once I got to college. Sho had made a name for himself at UNCG and started working at 102 Jamz. I looked up to him a lot. He told me to stay myself and to network my butt off, and I took his words to heart. I ended up choosing to attend North Carolina Central University (Durham, NC) for college. I must say, out of all the bad decisions I have made in my life this was probably one of the smartest ones I had made. It was a blessing from God. I graduated from Northeast Guilford High School with the bittersweet taste that my dad didn't see me cross the stage, but at least it gave me permission to leave Greensboro. Just like Simba left Pride Rock after Mufasa died, I was running away from the nightmare that my personal life had become. I was ready to stampede away.

Swiss was from Durham, NC and told me he knew some people he would plug me in to in order to make my transition easier. One day I had to take something to NCCU–like a transcript or something, and Swiss came down with me. While we were sitting in the student union he ran into another brother of Alpha Phi Alpha Fraternity, Inc. and helped networked me with him. His name was Corey Dinkins. Not only was Corey an Alpha man, but he was the newly crowned Mr. NCCU.

Around the same time, I had an old basketball teammate who was already at NCCU and he had made a name for himself. His name was Jerry Blackwell. Jerry or "J Black" is hands down the most talented MC that I know personally, and when he was not hooping he was destroying guys in the cafeteria in hip hop freestyle cyphers. But I looked up to him a lot, and I still do. He ran in Antonio's circle in high school and was doing really good for himself. He was really involved in the SGA at NCCU and knew that I had intentions of continuing my SGA involvement once I got to campus. He introduced me to a guy name Eric Jefferson, and Eric had just crossed Alpha the semester I came to campus. He and Corey immediately took to me for some odd reason.

Erika and Alicia at NE Prom   Tiara, Twin and I at Graduation

During my orientation at NCCU, one of my orientation leaders asked me if I was interested in doing anything my freshman year, and I told them I was interested in running for Freshman Class President. They told me I looked more like a Mr. Freshman. I wasn't familiar with the term, but I told Corey what happened and ironically enough he told me he had already known he wanted me to be a part of his royal court. He explained how each class has a king and queen that make up the royal court for the school. So, I agreed that it would be one of my goals. To me, I thought: "Well heck, at least it will give me a platform to help me promote parties," which I wanted to keep doing so I could pay for my tuition.

The underlying problem at the time was the fact that my mother and I were not on good terms, and when I filed for my financial aid to attend school, they made me go under my mother finances instead of DiDi's. My mother made too much money for me to receive any assistance. So, I knew I needed about $5,800 to make to through the semester and my aunt Laura had sent me about $2,500. I was able to have a good start at chopping down this bill. Swiss help set me up to throw the first party on campus with the brothers Alpha Phi Alpha which was pretty unheard of to be an incoming freshman. I plugged in enough to throw a party with the Alphas. I had met up with a guy name Harper (Not his real name but for the

82

sake of reflection I will use this name for it is not my intentions to look at our relationship in a negative way). Over the summer he and I both agreed to partner up to do parties. He was from Durham and thought how I thought when it came to doing parties. We did our first party at this place called the Marvell located in downtown Durham, and with the stamp from the Alphas, I went on a promoting storm to get people to the party. We packed the place out and "Prince" had arrived.

I loved being in Durham. People had no idea of who I was in regards to being Rev. King's son, and I didn't tell them either. If somebody asked my name, I referred to myself as Prince; no first name no last name... just Prince. I was able to make friends easily with my relationship with Corey and Eric. Corey plotted to make me Mr. Freshman before I even knew what the position was. I was introduced to the rest of the court weeks before the freshman elections and, he instructed everybody to embrace me to make it easier when it came to election time. So all of a sudden, I was this nobody incoming freshman from Greensboro who was hanging out with the who's who of NCCU.

Because Corey was Mr. NCCU, I was always in the place to be; skipping lines, sitting with the seniors, and before I knew it, I knew more upperclassmen than I did my own peers. I continued to throw parties and pay my own tuition. Although I was not as focus on my academics as I should have been, I made due. The night of speech and debate I knew one of my strong points were public speaking. I did a great job if I must say so myself.

My campaign manager was a girl name Timberly Butler, who was a twin and both her and her sister Tierra Butler was freshmen on Champagne–the NCCU cheerleading team. Timberly was almost a reflection of me, just in female form. Everyone was trying to pair us together, but we were just good friends. After the speech and debate night, word had spread around campus on how well I did but I was nervous for another reason...I had not paid my entire school bill. I knew the deadline was the same day the results came out.

I found out election night that I won the Mr. Freshman title and was overjoyed. The next day I found out that I had been dropped from all of my classes. So, I was crying all the way to the SGA office to tell the SGA advisor, Mrs. Robeson, that I wouldn't be able to stay in school. I ran into the SGA president from the year before Mukar Rakeb, and he told me that everything would be okay and walked with me the rest of the way. Once I got to Mrs. Robeson office and explained my situation with tears in my eyes. She smiled at me and said, "don't worry, we aren't going to lose our Mr. Freshman." They put me on scholarship for the rest of my time at NCCU. Mrs. Roberson passed away two years later, but she still holds a very special place in my heart and everyone's heart for that matter.

There was a big fashion show on campus that year for homecoming and we were throwing a party the next day but the host still talked about our party on stage. I had a late class, so I walked in about midway through the show and not ten minutes into my arrival they mentioned the party. The gym was packed, so I sat up at the top of the second level. While mentioning the party one host says, "Prince is going to be there, I know you all know Prince." I was floored, I've been used as an incentive to get people to come out to the party in front of a packed gym. Needless to say, I got a few "Hey big head" texts shortly afterward.

I was a part of the royal court now, and I could not have been more pleased with myself. I was already familiar with most of the court, but once I actually got elected, they welcomed me and my freshman queen Hope in with open arms. Hope herself is a trip. I had grew up with her in Greensboro and was just as proud to have her as my queen that year. Our Miss NCCU at the time was TT. She was always the proper politically correct one and use to always greet me with an enthusiastic, "My Prince!!" Chanel our Ms. Junior was the really sweet one who always checked on me, and our Ms. Sophomore Ashley was my buddy. We usually sat beside each other on bus trips and had great conversations.

Then, it was our Ms. Senior Sabrina, who at the time was probably pound for pound the most intimidating female on the yard. This information came from most of the females I spoke to about the subject matter. But I loved Sabrina, and all of our mean mug facial expressions. She looked out for me like big sister. Plus, I got more clout with females after they saw mean ole' Sabrina being nice to me. That was our female court, pretty, diverse, and on time. Then there was our male court.

In comparison, we always looked good, but being punctual wasn't always our strongest characteristic as the male court. There was our Mr. Sophomore, my boy Travis who was a laid back country boy with a funny sense of humor. Then it was John our Mr. Junior. John was my boy that I could always talk sports with, and I always admired his drive. Then it was Corey and Jacob Bagley or "Bags." Bags was an Omega. He and Corey were arguably the most well-known Greeks on the yard and they hung out all the time, and would take me with them.

Royal Court Moments Featuring Robert Townson

Bags was the life of the party. He would always get on the bus when we would have games with a green Gatorade water bottle and say, "Here Prince taste this." Without fail, my head would start spinning shortly after drinking a flavor that I KNOW Gatorade didn't approve of, unless there was a Hennessey flavor that I was unaware of. One time on a trip as a male court, we woke up super late Saturday morning after partying all night Friday, which was a problem because we were supposed to be at the Chancellor's breakfast early the next morning. As we rush to get ourselves together I remember Travis asking "where are the girls?" The ladies were already down stairs dressed and accounted for. I guess they were over being late on our behalf.

As we continued to gather ourselves on the elevator ride down, we did last minute "hangover" checks on each other to ensure we were presentable. The plan was to sneak into the back and just play the background until the end of the breakfast, except Corey opened the wrong door to the breakfast. Instead of opening a door in the back, he had opened the door in the front of the room. As soon as he opened the door he had made eye contact with the Chancellor who was up giving remarks. He instructed us to come in and join him, and we all bashfully entered the room as he remarked, "nice for the male court to finally join the party." And for the remainder of the time he spoke we stood behind him, subjected to the entire room's attention. But as embarrassed and hung over as we were, we still looked good. At the end of the day that's what counted as a win for the male court.

I had a group of friends that I started hanging with when I got to Central and we called our group "8 strong." It was eight of us who were arguably some of the most popular freshmen of our class. Our crew was legit. My boy Jason Bobbitt, who is now an actor for Tyler Perry; Harper, Charles, Dominique, Willis, DJ, Eric & myself. Just like all good things, it came to an end and we all we all separated into different circles. I decided to play the mutual friend to all of them. I got pretty cool with my roommate Jon too. He was from Charlotte and we could not have been more different.

Jon was dark skin, and I was light skin. He was a big Lil Boosie Fan, and I wasn't. I was a huge Jay-z fan and Jon was not. He was a UNC fan, and I was a Duke fan. I mean we couldn't have been more opposite, but we both had mutual respect for each other and held our room down. He was a great roommate. We stayed on the 8th floor in Eagleson Hall which was an upperclassmen hall. We were only allowed to stay there because we registered late for housing, but it ended up being a better situation. It built up the allure to our year.

That semester I had also developed a friendship with a guy name Brint. He and I had gotten acquainted by Swiss and their company at the time, Acapella Productions, was doing a lot of parties in the area. We partnered on the first party with the Alphas at the Marvell. To be honest, that night I was a little salty because Brint was doing most of the on mic hosting, which for a large extent had been my role at the party, but he was good and I recognized that. But for whatever reason, he and Harper did not really get along very well, at least well enough to continue to do parties together.

Party Hustling with Brint   My boy Dj Huggins

Brint stayed down the hall from me and I was always in his room. His roommate had left school early, so he had the room to himself. We stayed up a lot of nights plotting on stealing snacks from other girls rooms, playing Madden, and trying to get to the bottom of who killed his hamster (laugh out loud). But I always admired his grind and now he and his partner Tim are the top promoters in the RDU area. It was an honor to say that I came up with them. Shout out to my boy Marceau too, all love fam.

But, the one time I did have to go up against Brint was on my birthday that year and lines were drawn. It was Brint and his crew with the Ques against my 19th birthday, and to be fair I would say it wasn't fair. I had a plan. I called a few people I was doing parties with back in Greensboro. One of them was a guy name KB, and the other was a DJ I got connected with through E Sudd back in high school. His name was DJ Cuttz. One thing about me is when I use to throw parties, I always tried to separate myself from what other people were doing and since there was a big difference in the club markets of Greensboro and Durham, I felt like I was well prepared. There were a lot more clubs in Greensboro which was more of a party town. At any given night, there may be 4 or 5 parties going on throughout the city.

In Durham that was not the case. At most, you may have another party or two to compete against. I also met two other freshmen from NC A&T; Boss and Brav. They were similar to me in regards to young promoters doing big scale things. I had always had my cousin Droopy working with me. He and my boy Oct kept going what we started in high school. This gave me two markets to bring together. The idea was good... but the execution had to be better. Well not only did I have to compete with Brint, but the week before the party a Trey Songz party was announced and all of a sudden the stakes had risen. Brint was partnering with a party crew who had been around for some years prior to me arriving on campus called Legend Entertainment. They were not too fond of outsiders shaking the establishment, and of course, I was rocking the boat.

That week I called KB, and he got his promotion team CCU to partner on my birthday party which was kind of unheard of because my party was on a Thursday and they usually would have their own party going on in Greensboro. But my thinking was, 'well I might split crowds with Brint and may lose some girls to the Trey Songz party; but if I brought Greensboro to Durham that should make up for the difference.'

As the days approached, I realized we were doing pretty well on our pre-sale tickets, which was a very encouraging sign. The day of the party it seemed as if I was selling tickets all day. This sometimes could be an illusion because presale tickets only make up about 20% of our attendance. We had this down to a science, or at least we thought. Before the party, I decided to go against my usual party routine which was to be one of the first at the clubs to ensure that everything was running smoothly. Instead, I went to pregame at Corey's apartment because Kiara and our friend Erica came into town to celebrate with me. Of course, my phone dies and after a few drinks I am feeling pretty good about my birthday. Then we get a call that we should get to the club as soon as possible.

I wasn't what you would call sober at the time, so I did not understand what was quite going on and I thought something terrible had happened at the party. But as we finally pulled up to the club, I began to notice cars parked far away from the club which was a very good sign. I myself had almost 20 people with me so it made me feel like a celebrity getting out of the car with everyone. As I walked up to the club, my eyes grew larger with every step I took. It seems like the entire school was at this party. I mean it was so many people it took me back and I was used to having big crowds for my party, but this was ridiculous.

I finally was able to make it to the door and Harper told me that the Brint party had shut down and Trey Songz was told to turn around even before he made it to Durham. My birthday party won (to be fair, Brint's anniversary shut my party down two weeks later, but that was the sport of party promotion, you win some and you lose some). Walking into the party I could see KB and Cuttz in the DJ booth rocking, and after I received my birthday shout outs, for a moment I really felt like Mitch from Paid in Full walking around the club. I finally took a seat, a seat in which I did not get up from for the rest of the night and just enjoyed being Prince.

KB MistaGetItPoppin   CCU

The only picture of myself I could find   Best Bday Party Ever

And once again, I apologize for anyone who couldn't get in that night, there were circumstances that were out of my control. Because I was focused on everything but class, I made a 1.9 GPA that semester. Gratefully, we had one of the best kick-in-the-butts by SGA President, Mr. Tomasi Larry. Tomasi basically told me I was underachieving, and I needed to get my act together in so many words (laugh out loud). The next semester I made a 3.7 GPA. I was determined not to go back to Greensboro, so I realized I had to buckle down on my studies so I could stay in Durham as long as possible. I settled into life in Durham. I rarely went back to Greensboro, and I didn't have much contact with anyone from Greensboro either. I was satisfied with being "Prince," no first name...no last name, just "Prince."

I always took great pride in walking into the cafeteria by myself and being able to sit and talk with all the different circles on campus. Whether it was with the athletes or the cheerleaders, the dance crews or modeling troops, girls sitting by themselves or any of the Black Greeks; I took job as Mr. Freshman serious in regards to networking. I told myself I wouldn't meet a stranger and that I wouldn't purposely create enemies.

I will always appreciate what Corey did for me. He took me under his wing and although I was hard headed in the beginning, the things he taught me gave me the foundation to build my college career. Corey would come by the front of the Student Union where most of the freshman and other underclassmen hung out at and yell, "Prince come ride with me." To me, as a freshman at NCCU, there was no cooler experience than to have Mr. NCCU seek you out amongst the crowd. Girls especially paid close attention to the attention I was getting from upperclassmen, and I like the attention they were giving me for it.

One time we had traveled to with the football team to Savannah and we were in the hotel the night before the game. Let's just say Corey and I was doing something we weren't supposed to be doing. As we finished up, we walked back to the hotel only to be cornered by the elevator and the Chancellor of NCCU at the time. Worried about "our smell," with no hesitation we both jetted up the steps racing neck to neck all the way up to the 4th floor and passed out by our rooms. We get a good giggle out of that story every time it was brought up. We really dodged a bullet that night. In a certain way, Corey had been the big brother I was searching for, somebody I could vent to without any worry of judgment, and I knew that I would be receiving some sound advice in return.

Eric and I shared a different brotherhood experience than Corey and I, but it was just as fulfilling. As Corey and I were on the Royal Court, Eric was the Junior Class President and had one of the most successful and active class council to date during my time at NCCU. Eric was a natural leader who was wise beyond his years. He had a mean temper to go along with it, but we all knew that was just Eric. Corey and Eric were the two stabilizing forces for me in Durham. They were the first two people I met in Durham and we end up becoming lifelong friends. Shout out to Jacob Bagley too; my Mr. Senior; he also had a major impact on me.

Chapter Seven: Hood Politics

Streets don't fail me now, they tell me it's a new gang in town
From Compton to Congress, set Trippin' all around
Ain't nothin' new, but the flu of new Demo-Crips and
Re-Blood-licans
Red state versus a blue state, which one you governin'?
They give us guns and drugs, call us thugs
Make it they promise to f&^k with you
No condom they f*&k with you, Obama say, "What it do?"

-Kendrick Lamar (Hood Politics)

Chris Rivers, Faith Bynum and myself with former Gov. Pat McCrory

I established a relationship with a guy name Mr. Keith in the café at NCCU; that was my buddy. We would always speak to each other and encourage each other to have the best week possible. Sometimes Mr. Keith would let me come in the café in the summer when I didn't have a meal plan... talk about clutch. But one day I was walking to class and Mr. Keith stopped me in front of the football stadium. He had run to catch up with me, and I could tell he had something pressing to tell me. He told me that the day before he was at church and they were having an altar call. He was just standing there praying and all of a sudden God gave him a vision of me speaking in front of what he said was an endless crowd of people. He told me he knew at that moment, I am going to do something great with my life. I think we had that conversation my sophomore year. From then on he always referenced the vision he had for me in our conversations. Leaving me to think... 'wow... I wonder what God has planned for me?

Going into my sophomore year a new phenomenon was occurring; a black man was running for President. That entire summer of 2008, my eyes were glued to the television to learn as much as I could about this guy with a strange name, Barack Obama. This had totally taken over my interest beyond anything else I was involved with, and I wanted to do anything I could to help him win. A small part of me knew that if my father was alive that that would be exactly what he would have been doing; Helping Barack Obama win. That fall when Senator Obama came to our campus to speak. I was amazed at the diversity that came out to hear him. It wasn't just black people, it was Asians, Whites., Blue, and Green. Everybody wanted to hear what he had to say. He was such a dynamic speaker.

By this time Prince was in full swing around campus and I was gaining somewhat of a reputation and depending on what environment you were talking about, you would get a different response. I was getting a lot of attention, and I was taking full advantage of it. I remember there was a time when I was a chubby kid who couldn't get girls to look my way so adjusting to the female attention was a learning curve, to say the least. In the midst of the campus fame, I was dealing with a lot of women–a lot of women.

Lovely/Angry Alpha Chi

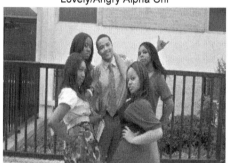

My DMV Buddies

If I was not dealing with a female on our campus, it was a female on the campus of NCST, Duke, UNC Chapel Hill, and any other female that I might have met on other campuses or at my parties. My parties were the catalyst for a lot of my relations with females. I never was quite sure if they were really interested in me or the fact that I would let them and their friends skip line and get in for a discount (never for free). For whatever reason the ladies loved Prince... and Prince loved the ladies.

But it cost me as well. During my heyday, I messed over

a lot of good women, but I would like to say that I was always respectful. Now that I have a daughter, I would like to apologize to Sparkle, B Brown, Dr. C James, S Pittman and especially Princess Barnes. Princess Barnes was a lady that I went to highschool with who was two years older than I was. She meant a lot to me.

Once she graduated, she went to UNCG and use to work in a hospital, and I went to go hang with her as much as I could. We were always friends coming up and although I had the biggest crush on her when I finally got my opportunity to move towards a relationship (which was what I always wanted) I found out that I had a daughter. I was too ashamed to tell her and ended up losing out on a really amazing person. Although God has shown me favor and has blessed me with a woman who I now understand I was made to be with, it makes it easier to move on.. but not easy to realize you played with a lot of hearts to finally get to learn your lesson. So like Jay-Z said, "I pray that I am forgiven for every bad decision I made… every sister afterward played… because I am still paranoid until this day, and it's nobody's fault. I made the decisions I made… this is the life I chose… or rather the life that chose me."

Over the course of the second semester, I also assimilated into another group of friends. They called themselves the "Fly Boyz." They were mostly a group of sophomores who were considered the coolest freshmen the year prior. I had connected with one of the main guys Tremaine or Tre Holla. He was the Mr. Freshman the year prior, but we never got to spend as much time building together as I had wished. I also cherished my friendship with Tre because of the example he set for me to follow. Compared to my "8 strong" crew, the "Fly Boyz" were even bigger. Trap, Petey Crack, Mackie, Dev, Tre, Man Man, Ryan, Free, Laflare, Antonio and a few more; those were my boys. Our group was certainly one of if not the most known group of guy friends in the underclassmen classifications. We even had a hand shake.

Tremain   Travis

They were the first group of guys that I felt comfortable to opened up to, and that was significant to me due to the characteristic nature of "Prince." I was mysterious and purposely so. I did not want to talk about my past or anything sensitive so other people saw it as I use to lie a lot. I saw it as keeping people out of my business… I was a campus figure… so it wasn't as if people weren't interested in my story. I just wasn't interested in telling it at the time. By that summer, I had a heart to heart with the Fly Boyz, and we all talked about our life experiences. This would be the first time I would disclose anything about, "Matthew."

The funny thing is a few days later Rod came to me and told me another guy there came to him afterward to say that my story had checked out. I guess my story was so unbelievable that they had to Google it for themselves. I always wondered if they took time out to fact check everyone else's story as well. That moment put me right back in my feelings about why I had to be Prince in the first place because no one would believe me if I would have told them any way that I was Matthew King, son of Famous Rev. Michael King. I couldn't prove it… not materially, anyway.

That fall a guy name AJ Donaldson, who was an upperclassman and an Alpha man, had organized a group called the Obama Squad and invited me to be a part of the team. The Obama campaign had sent celebrities to the campus to campaign for President Obama, and I was able to host almost all the events. I got to meet Raven Symone, Tatyana Ali, Jurnee Smollett, and Fonzworth Bentley. It was certainly a once and a lifetime experience. We lead a march the first day of early voting and it seems as if the entire campus had come out to vote.

Obama Squad   Eric, Kent, Dwayne and myself at Aggie/Eagle Classic

Politics as Usual   Jurnee Smollett-Bell

    I had met two guys named Dwayne Johnson and Josh Spells, who had intentions of becoming a member of Alphas Phi Alpha Fraternity, Inc. and we ended up rooming together that semester. Dwayne had won Sophomore Class President, and Josh was a part of NCCU's drumline DOXA (one of the baddest in the land), and we stayed in the infamous 254 room in Ruffin Hall. We created another brotherhood bond between the three of us; holding each other accountable to make sure we were doing well in college and having fun while we were at it. Josh and I were the playboys while Dwayne was the good guy helping bring the girls to our room.

    It's always funny for me to hear Dwayne explain how we

met because he would be the first to admit he did not like me freshman year. He would say, "Man, I would be around girls and all I would hear is, Prince this and Prince that." Little did we know we would be making the remaining memories of college at each other's hip. Josh and I didn't really know each other our freshman year, but we knew of each other. Once we finally got to know each other we became family. Both Josh and Dwayne's families took me in as their own. When they brought things for Josh or Dwayne, they would triple what they bought so I could have some too... and I loved them for that.

Dwayne and I had come up with an event to incorporate on campus to help freshman understand what campus life was all about. We came up with an event called "Training Day." It was our first big trademark event on campus, and we wanted to stamp ourselves as campus leaders. It took us about two months to get the event together and I even called Sho Smoove to come up from Greensboro to help host it. The event was a huge success and to this day, NCCU still does the Training Day event at the start of the year for freshmen to get them acclimated to campus life.

I remember not enjoying my freshman year orientation experience because of the event that we had, so I wanted to create an event to take the place of it. I felt that the event should have had more production and a better spin. With the help of G Baby and She-She, we were able to set the groundwork for what would become a staple event in the NCCU orientation experience. We scheduled the event in the evening, and we held it on the Thursday evening before the last day of freshman orientation. The concept behind the event was to get all the organizations an opportunity to introduce themselves to the freshman but to do it in a cooler way than how it was presented to me. I just always been that type of person, if I don't like something I don't complain about it, I just begin to think about how to replace it with a solution. Training day had been bubbling in my mind all freshman year and the sight of a black man running for President encouraged me to try to bridge the gap between not only just being a popular student on campus but also using my platform to advocate for issues that affect the student body.

Eric and I also worked to bring the first Midnight Madness to campus. It was a great event to be able to plan with the first year basketball coach Levell Moton. The event was well intended even though it was the first time, and it was over fall break weekend. The boys' basketball team did a New Edition rendition that was really good. We had some of the Black Greeks to step and had 97.5 helped us bring the community out; much love to radio personality, Brian Dawson. I remember the trips that I took as a part of the SGA my first two years. At all the football games and college events, I was all about promoting NCCU. I was able to create a separate identity based off of myself and I was pleased with the results. That year I had hosted the homecoming step show with Eric who had become Mr. NCCU after Corey, and it was the week before the presidential election.

The week of the election Eric and I walked down to the gas station down the street from the school and saw Obama shirts with his face made out of metals that outlined his face. We immediately knew those were the shirts we were going to wear in the show. During the show, I had a moment that I asked everyone in the crowd to hold up "O" in a hand sign and I told the DJ to drop Young Jeezy's, "My President is Black," and it was like you could feel the entire gym rock. That moment will stay with me for the rest of my life. The night before the election you could feel a nervous tension in our Obama Squad session because we knew we had put so much work in, we were sure that someway somehow they would figure out how to steal the election. That fueled us to work nonstop through the night. Days before we had a huge march to the polls during early voting... it felt like we had the entire campus with us. But after we saw the voting numbers, we realize we still had much more work to do. The day of the election we were still making sure we could get as many people to the polls as we could, and I can honestly say that was the first time that I could remember that it wasn't cool if you didn't vote. NCCU ended up having 97% of our campus to vote. This was by far more than any other school in the UNC school system. Our Eagle Pride is always amplified!

Eric and I hosting the step show

That night it was a huge watch party in the student union, and everyone was nervous watching the results. I think that was because of the Bush elections of 2000. But when they finally announced that he had won, it was like you could hear the entire campus explode. People started going crazy, it was the biggest campus party I had ever been a part of. Even at the height of excitement, I had to take a few seconds to myself and shed a tear or two because if my father was here to see it he would be proud. After I got myself together, I joined my peers in the celebration. We were in the middle of the street stopping traffic just having the biggest party you would ever want to see. This was one the best experiences of my life.

Chapter Eight: *Sacrifices*

And I done sacrificed my own time
I done sacrificed my own mind
I done sacrificed the club life
I done sacrificed my love life

Big Sean (Sacrifices)

The next semester I took my journey to become a member of Alpha Phi Alpha Fraternity Incorporated. What made the journey so sweet was the fact that I was able to do it with Dwayne and Josh... but I also gained 14 line brothers that I love to death and back: Marko, Steven, RJ, Quintin, Arthur, Mark, Dwayne, Zach, Josh, Katona, Rasheed, Roddrick, Nealie, and Jerrin. My 14 line brothers helped me grow up and mature as a man. Until this day if you bring all of us together, you'd be asking for a party to be started; I love those boys.

Marko was from Maryland and is the biggest Go-Go music fan I know. He was always trying to put me up on the newest Go-Go mixtape, but he was our leader. I was the wild child out of the bunch. Steven was a medical genius who is at Harvard Medical School and MIT obtaining his PhD and M.D right now and one of the more musically inclined people I know. RJ was a country boy who was wise beyond his years. We are both big Duke fans. Quintin was the understood crazy one out of the group. He was so mild tempered but would show flashes of insanity that would frighten all of us (laugh out loud).

I looked up to Quintin the most out of my brothers. Arthur was older and was pretty much one of the punch lines to everybody's jokes. This guy is a character, but he was and is a great influence on us and he has shown us the importance of being a man. Mark was the odd one out of the group to say the least. He was a bit of a book worm, bit of a music head, and definitely had a huge heart. Mark would be the one who got us in trouble the most.

Dwayne was our voice of reason. We all looked to Dwayne to provide his logical perspective on things. Zach was the youngest and wildest behind me. He was on the football team and is one of the most reliable people I know. Josh was the line spokesman and step master; two of the higher honors a person could hold. Josh was the face of the line in many aspects. Katona was the rock of the line. To this day Katona is the glue that holds us all together. If I hadn't talked to one of my LBs in a while and I can't get a hold of him, I can just called Katona. More than likely Katona would have the most recent update on my LB. Rasheed was the oldest, and he set the standard of success for us. Because he graduated the same semester we crossed, we only got to spend a limited amount of time with him on campus. He showed us that it was more than just throwing parties and programs. He encouraged us to make something out of our college experience that would translate into a career.

Rod was one of my freshman year homeboys who has one of the most epic stories of overcoming the struggles of life. Anytime I think that I have something to complain about, I always remember Rod's story and how much he had to overcome to fulfill his dreams; he is an conquer.

Gamma Beta   IDD

Nealie on the other hand, was the muscle of the line. when Nealie was around, he just had a presence about him that made you feel safe and was author to most of our inside jokes. He was the biggest in size and turned out to be an all-time great for NCCU track and field. Jerrin was the Tallest and the loudest one of us all. Jerrin was always my buddy even prior to us becoming line brothers. I always admired how he stayed so loyal to all of his obligations on campus, and he did it with so much passion.

But at the end of the day the one thing we are all the most proud of is the that every one of us received our college degrees. It was one of the top goals we set for ourselves. During our process one night I had a dream that I will not disclose, but I went back and told my line brothers about it and we went to our older brothers and told them about my dream. Although initially, they just brushed my dream under the rug, two weeks later what I dreamed about actually came true and that's how I got my line name "Daniel" from the bible. Daniel had the power of God speaking through him in his dreams. I could relate to Daniel a lot.

At the end of my sophomore year in college I had accomplished and seen more than most people had in the entire four years of their undergraduate experience. But yet, my story took another unexpected twist. The next year I knew my little sister Bethany was coming to college and would face some of the same financial problems that I had coming to college. So, I decided to join the military. I didn't announce it or consult with a lot of people about it. As a matter of fact, most people didn't know that I was leaving until the day before I left. So, instead of enjoying what was supposed to be the glory days of college I was off to Fort Knox Kentucky for basic training… not understanding at all what I was getting myself into.

When I arrive to Fort Knox, I was excited and nervous at the same time. I had heard stories about basic training, and I wondered how I would fair in that environment. The one thing that I did understand was there was no turning back. I was assigned to Delta 245 with Drill Sergeant Johns, Stevens, and Gilmore; and it was such a culture shock for me. I had never lived with such a diverse group of people in my life... people from all around the world. It opened my eyes to how big the world really was. I remember one morning sitting on my bag and looking up at the sky asking God, "what did I get myself into?" I was trying to stay strong, but the culture was really different.

I was blessed to have very good Drill Sergeants, especially Drill Sergeant Johns. He was a sniper and was really young to be ranked as high was he was. He was so cool, he never yelled or lost control but he demanded respect and excellence. In the military there is a term called "smoked," which is corrective training where they exercise to the point of death to whip you back in shape. One particular day we were being smoked, and he stopped and asked the group why weren't we hitting the learning curve? As far as he thought we should have. I raised my hand and said, "It's because we have some weak minded people." Anthony Jones who was from Arkansas spoke up and echoed my same sentiments and right after that Sergeant Johns appointed Jones PG and me APG which is the leaders of the Platoon. We took the jobs from two white guys who didn't really take well to two black guys being in charge. Almost overnight you could see a difference in our platoon.

Jones was the level headed leader that got along with everybody, and I was his Pitbull that kept everybody in line. We physically were one of the more gifted soldiers in the group, so we had their respect in that regard. The leadership part was something we had to work on. Jones and I mode of operation was not to show favoritism to anyone; excellence was expected from everybody. There were two more platoons that made up the company, so we were in constant competition to win any and everything. Drill Sergeant Johns was very competitive, and we wanted nothing more than to please him.

He saw that we won the respect of our peers and as we continued basic training, we renewed the spirit of not only making it through but excelling at all the tasks we were given.

At the same time the only communication we were able to have were the letters that people sent to us and a 5 minute conversation on Sunday. During that time, my mother and I started writing letters to each other and were able to hash out our differences and agreed to start anew; which was very important to me. Although I enjoyed the experience of basic training it did end on a sour note because a few days before graduation our platoon had earned Honor Platoon for being the highest performing platoon.

My boy Bell and Dowdy

Under Jones and I leadership meant that Jones and I were going to be the two soldiers leading the company into graduation which was a big honor. Drill Sergeant Johns called us into his office and told us that he was making the original two white guys PG and APG again and thanked us for our leadership and that was it. Jones and I were hurt, but we understood that some things still had not changed much. Almost all of our platoon was upset about what happen but we got over it because we knew that at the end of the day, we were about to leave Fort Knox and that was what was most important. The day we left Fort Knox to go to our next base for AIT training we were in the airport on September 11th. I had never been so proud to be an American Soldier. We had on our ACU's and everyone was so kind to us. Random people were stopping us and thanking us for our service, buying us lunch, and even allowing us to fly first class on the flight. It was another experience that will stay with me for the rest of my life.

Once I got to Fort Sill Oklahoma for AIT training, I was comfortable about my decision with leaving school for the military, but I was ready to get back to school. I enjoyed my time in Oklahoma for what it was worth. I met some good people and really had fun on the weekends. My military job was in artillery, and we were to coordinate firing points for the guns bunnies to shoot at. Essentially we were the first to be put on ground for our company and it was up to us to make sure bombs made it to their correct target. One concept that we had to learn is how to coordinate the stars to do our job in the event our GPS system went down. This started my love for gazing at the stars. I had a total spiritual experience looking at the stars at night admiring the awesomeness of God with such imagination to create something so massive and so breathtaking.

There would be nights in the field when we would be on duty watch and you could hear the coyotes roaming in the back. There were three guys that use to chill like me; Bell, Dowdy, and Blocker. Bell and Dowdy was from D.C area, Dowdy was a true representation of his city to say the least. This guy always had me laughing. Bell and I had gone to boot camp together and use to work out and play basketball a lot. Blocker was from Alabama and was as country as it gets. He and I had a good relationship and would usually be the ones cutting out on break.

I really enjoyed my time at Ft. Sill. At the time I was really ready to get back home, but the memories that I have will last me forever. I was blessed to come in contact with some very genuine and some not so genuine people. One in particular would be my sergeant. Sergeant Heard was a brother who initially gave me a hard time because he thought I was some crazy frat boy, but we grew to have a good bond. I would end up being the soldier he would always call to be his co-driver anywhere he went. He only wanted me there to talk junk to me but we also talked about life and getting the most out of it. What I can appreciate about him the most was that he never came off like a know-it-all or someone who was extremely superior to you. He was very approachable. His door was always opened for me and he helped me graduate AIT, and for that, I will be forever grateful.

I graduated from Fort Sill and made my way back to Durham to start school again. I was welcomed back with open arms, and to a certain extent I received even more admiration for my decision to leave for the military. It was a blessing from God because there was times when I was gone that I questioned whether or not I made the right decision. But I had my little sister in Durham with me, and I could finally enjoy my college experience without any interruption... or at least I thought.

Chapter Nine: *Nightmares from the Bottom*

Okay, I'm walking on needles, sticking to the point
Yeah the streets is talking, I'm familiar with the voice
I'm a gangsta by choice, I hope my sons choose wiser
And don't call me "Sir," call me "Survivor"

-Lil Wayne (Nightmares from the bottom)

I was able to come back and move in with two of my homeboys from Greensboro, my boy Lundon, and Omari. I grew up with Omari and played on many basketball teams with him, he was a hoop star in high school and a real solid guy (still grateful for your mom). Omari and Lundon had gone to highschool together. Although I didn't meet Lundon until college we immediately connected and had a lot in common… girls included. There were a few females that got caught up once he and I moved into together (laugh out loud). But that was my guy, we spend many days betting on 2k and laughing at Omari jokes. I felt as if I was finally able to enjoy college.

By this time Ish had transferred up to NCCU, and Harper and I had begun throwing parties together. We were very successful too. Ish and I had common ideas about how to execute the parties with us both being from Greensboro. Harper was the hometown person and had pledged Kappa so by default, every one of our parties had some Kappa and Alpha influence. We shared a brotherhood together through all the time we spent creating and executing these ideas. Dwayne had become SGA President, and I used hosting events on campus and my influence to leverage our promotion for our parties. Most of the promoters in the area were from the area, and I wasn't so I had to use creative ways to be competitive. I was usually the official "after party" promoter as well.

Another card I used was having access to basketball players from UNC. Will Graves and I kept in contact throughout college, and there would be times that he would call me because he had recruits in town and he wanted to show them a good time. Although it was usually against my religion to help the Tar Heels do anything, Will was my boy, so they got the red carpet treatment when they came. I ended up getting to meet Harrison Barnes, John Henson, and a few more guys even prior to their first game at UNC, and way before they became NBA stars.

That year Bethany had won Ms. Freshman, and I don't know how many times that has happen in Royal Court history, but I was very proud of her. It wasn't easy walking in my shadows and I made sure that she earned the title on her own merit, and she did. I was so proud to watch her be crowned as Ms. Freshman, way more than I ever could of my own Mr. Freshman victory. I was always concerned how about her self-esteem would be because I knew of my own self-esteem issues that I was dealing with. But it was always unspoken language between Prince and BeKay, NCCU had given us a second chance.

Miss Freshman BeKay   Lance Thomas

That semester Duke had won the National Championship in basketball. It was like a dream come true, and to be able to experience that first hand while in college was amazing. The year before UNC had won the championship and Franklin Street was ridiculous, but that year it was our turn. I remember watching the game at my line brother RJ house with some other fraternity brothers, and after the game was over, we raced in our cars to Ninth Street and went to the BP gas station right beside the campus. Could you believe that the entire beer section was sold out? So we left and ran to Duke's campus to join the celebration. I had been a Duke basketball fan for so long... so to actually be able to help throw benches in the bonfire was a surreal moment for me.

The next day, a few of us went over to hang out with Lance Thomas who was the starting power forward that year. After a while of being in his apartment someone knocks on his door... and in walks in Nolan Smith, Kyle Singler, and Jon Scheyer. I was blown away! I was actually with the Duke players literally less than 24 hours after they won the national championship. This was certainly a moment I will cherish for the rest of my life. Around the same time, I had also decided that I would become a high school History teacher and I wanted to coach basketball with no intentions of going back to Greensboro; ever if I could help it.

The next September my older brother Malachi was released from prison and the first night he was home, the three siblings sat up all night and caught up on the last 7 years that we had missed in each other's life... which was eerie considering the fact that no one could predict that Rev. King's children would have to grow up separate. But that night was the first night we were all together since our father's funeral. The transition was rough for my brother. I could see how prison had taken a toll on his mind. He was struggling with the fact that everything he once knew was not the same, and since he was an adult when my father died he had an understanding of the situation that Beth and I didn't have.

One person in particular that he brought to my attention was a man name DJ Ward. Ward was a pastor from the Kentucky/Tennessee area who had mentored my father early on in his ministry. He had also taken in my mother as an extended family early on after her college years. He was so close to our family I had perceived him to be my grandfather. I would not find out the truth about my mother's father until a few years later. And then Malachi dropped a truth bomb on me that changed my entire outlook on my existence. He told me that my father initially was dating my mother's best friend and that it was Ward's vision of my parents getting together more than it was their vision, and to a certain extent I am the product of an arranged marriage.

Malachi had been old enough to understand the influence Pastor Ward had on my Dad. He said he could remember the changes from the name of my dad's church, to the way my father wore his clothes, and even started my dad out on smoking pipes. I remember Malachi asking me, "Do you think it was strange that Pop had hundreds of suits, and all of them were Black?" It had never crossed my mind that every time my dad told me to gather his suits for the cleaners that he did not have any color but black, and that was out of hundreds of suits.

Malachi had told me that over time Pastor Ward and my father had a falling out. It was speculated that my father was becoming too popular and powerful for Ward's liking. The situation ended in my father telling Pastor Ward he would never step foot into his church ever again. Then Malachi and I spoke about the members of the church who had been conspiring against my father, and I am pretty sure they would be surprised about how much we know. The pinnacle of betrayal happens shortly after my father's death when those same members brought Pastor Ward back to my father's church.

According to a few people who I spoke to about that day, they were furious with the remarks Ward had made standing in my Father's pulpit, words that would be the ultimate divide of my Father's church. Pastor Ward stood up and said, "Man said that I would never step foot in this building again, but Look at God." Now I was not there to hear that, and thankfully I wasn't. That was disrespect on a totally different level, and those who my father thought loved him gave Ward the platform to be disrespectful. At the end of the day, people are only people I guess. Everyone's personal agenda was exposed, and ultimately smaller churches were made from my father's church. I always had a funny relationship with my brother, and in a lot of ways I looked up to him. I always joked that between Beth and Malachi, I felt like I was stuck between the Bush Twins. They indeed had a much closer relationship than I did with either of them growing up. They would constantly invite me to come watch TV with them, and I would constantly ignore them and go to my room. But I love the way he can carry his demeanor. He always had the flyest wardrobe, and he sort of felt like the closest I would get to witnesses how my grandfather operated. My brother adored my grandfather, and most of the history I know about him comes from my brother.

He was young enough to have lived on Benbow Street when the entire family still stayed there. He would say every morning he would wait for my grandfather to walk past his house and he would be waiting on the porch for him. My grandfather being a former army captain would say, "Where is my Lieutenant?" Malachi said that use to make his day. Apparently, somewhere down our Liberian roots we are related to a famous warlord turned pastor Joshua Blahyi (aka General Buttnaked). My brother told me when he was younger my grandfather used to love to tease him, and he would pick him up to tickle him and act as if he was going to eat his stomach saying, "Imma feed you to Buttnaked" (laugh out loud).

Malachi in all fairness did not have a particular easy childhood growing up. Dad had split with his mom and he came to stay with him. I always noticed my mom was not particularly as nice to him as she was to Bethany and I. that always kind of bothered me. Now in fairness to everyone else, Malachi was forever getting in trouble to where I only got a handful of spankings my entire life. He would get a handful of spankings every weekend. I think another factor that attributed to this though was the fact that he was 9 years older than me and was able to experience our family's wealth from a different perspective. I always wondered what it would have been like to go through high school and college with all the things I use to have growing up, but then again, by that time Malachi's incidents probably would have put things on lockdown for Beth and I.

I can recall us going out of town for a weekend and Malachi stayed behind at the house. And of course, while we were gone, he has women and all other type of lord knows what going on in the house. Now by this time he had been caught before having girls in the Jacuzzi, skipping late night school to go promote club parties, and the list goes on. But this particular time he felt as if he had cross all his T's and dotted all of his I's. He even took my mom's Mercedes to the gas station to fill up the tank and took his time to ever so perfectly put it back in the same spot she parked it in. Only two small details he failed to account for; one my mother's car took diesel, and he filled it up with lead and two, he left the sunroof open and it had rained later that night. Needless to say, when we returned my mother found her car filled with rainwater and leaves and an engine that was now in need of deep repair. I think it would also go without saying that my dad hit the roof.

Another time for his birthday, Malachi decided to treat himself to his birthday at my dad's expense. Now before I disclose what I am about to say, I myself wondered what in the hell my brother was thinking as well. That being said, he woke up on the day of his 18th birthday and was at the mall before it even opened and for whatever reason he had my dad's personal credit card. Now let him tell it, they had some sort of agreement that he could get a few things for his birthday. Those few things turned into a $8,000 dollar bill. Now let him explain it, and it's going to sound like the most amazing hip hop music video you have ever seen, he had his boys with him and they shut the mall down!!

Well, he says that about two months go by without my dad saying anything so he thinks he is in the clear. And then one day he showed up to work at Project Homestead, and he said as soon as he walked into the conference room to greet my dad, my dad was opening up his credit card bill. Malachi said the more he read the more he saw flames shoot up in my dad's eyes. He said he was so mad he didn't know what to do to him so he reverted back to his old wrestling and suplexed him. (Laugh out loud)

But that is the type of guy my brother has always been; a live at the moment and worry about the consequences later type of guy. He has always had the gift of singing. He use to tell me about him and his best friends, who were cousins, linked up with a Greensboro producer name Ski Beats. Ski Beats use to let them carry his records, one of them being Reasonable Doubt. Malachi swears if he ever ran into Jay-Z he could make him remember when they met, or maybe he was going on another Kanye rant, you could never tell with Malachi.

Malachi and I

After he left the house he went out to make it in the music industry, something he knew my father did not approve of. In the midst of everything, he was also sucked into the street life so much so that it overcame his identity as being Rev. King's son as well; just not as positively as Prince did for Matthew. He was a part of Tree Top Piru, and I was amazed at how much of the history he knew about his organization. I mean taking it back to Bobby Seale and Huey P. Newton. My biggest gripe with him was why not teach that history instead of allowing the young ones to just roam around blind. But I dearly wanted more for my brother. I hated to see what prison had done to him as a man, he had spent majority of his adult life locked up.

To a certain extent I felt like the older brother in many ways because it always felt as if he was trying to play catch up on all the fun that he missed out on. Without saying too much, I will just say that hanging around my brother he had me in some interesting environments to say the least. But he was my brother, and it always seemed as if he was the black sheep of the family. The one no one really wanted to deal with and some of that was self-inflicted, but I didn't care I just wanted to be there for my brother and do whatever I could to make sure he didn't go back to jail.

People he would introduce me to would always ask "What are you doing around your brother," not as much as in a demeaning way, but we were that much polar opposites in a lot of ways. To myself, I would always think, 'well Jesus hung out with the pushers and the pimps so why can't I?' Is my brother not human because of his decisions, and as a brother should I not try to at least show him a different route prior to passing off judgement? He was happy to be around me again, and I was happy to finally be back around him.

My brother contemplated going to the military as well, but I talked him out of it. At the same time I saw him go from job to job trying to find work, only to be shut down after his background check came back. I told him that if he would let me get pass the academic school year, I would help him start his music career; my brother is a gifted singer and always has been. I remember every time he sung in church growing up he would tear the church up. The most powerful moment of my dad's funeral was him being locked up in chains in his oversize suit with two policemen between them as he stood up and sang. I still remember seeing one of the officers wiping the tears from his eyes. I was confident that his voice would make him millions.

I was working four jobs at that time. One in Ladies shoes at Belks, third shift at circle K, I was working on campus at the VA office, and I was still in the military. That March I made a huge mistake and failed a drug test... but I was a good soldier and my captain liked me so I was going to get a slap on the wrist. He told me if I failed another drug test I would receive a general discharge. At the time I only knew of dishonorable and honorable discharge, so after he explained what a general discharge was it was my opportunity to cut my ties with the military and try to go strike it rich with my brother. The next drill I asked for a general discharge and was granted one, and that brought my military career to a close.

I saved my tax refund checks, sold my car, and made a few connections. After the year ended, we ventured out to hit the road to get Malachi a record deal. We hit Atlanta, Nashville, Myrtle Beach, and everywhere in between to try to get this record deal. These trips in my head were the beginning of an unforeseen future for myself. There was a point where I questioned if I even needed to finish my degree at that time, but in my head it was time to make some serious money. I was ready to assume my Dame Dash role in my brother's camp, and I ran full steam ahead.

We began booking studio time and live performances. I was utilizing NCCU as a platform to get his music out and he was receiving rave review, but a part of me was unsure about my brother's mental health to handle the pressures of being a music star. I could see he was still hurting. We made a lot of progress and we also made a lot of connections, but it seemed as if we could never get over the hump. He recorded one particular song called "Prisoner's Pray." It was a musical insight to his life and still hands down one of the greatest songs I have ever heard, and people who heard it more times than not agreed. I remember one day we were in downtown Greensboro driving, and he saw Fantasia Barrino walking out of some appearance she was having. Malachi quickly parked the car try to catch her before she left.

Now he had parked the car almost two blocks from

where she was, and I was more aware about the fact that he really left the car parked in the middle of the street. It was quite dangerous. After I pulled the car in a correct parking space, I finally caught up with my brother who at this point was all hugged up with Fantasia, and you could hear her say "How you doing with your singing self?" Growing up, Fantasia's church in High Point would come to our church to sing and she and my brother had known about each other for years. It felt pretty cool to see my brother get positive spotlight and not someone always talking down about him. I really wanted to see my brother obtain his dreams of singing. I always felt kind of self-conscious of the fact that I was always sort of an over-achiever. I just wanted to see people talk about him the same way they talked about me.

Malachi in LA at Game Studio   Yung Berg and Malachi

My ultimate goal was to link Malachi with one of my fraternity brothers, Harvey Cummings. Harvey was the first Mr. NCCU ever, and he and I developed a good relationship prior to him leaving campus. He had also made quite a name for himself as a musician playing the piano and the saxophone. He was going to be the perfect complement to for Malachi's talent. To Malachi's credit, he had also started to make a name for himself performing and even won an X-Factor competition in Greensboro, I was super proud of him.

We ended up settling in Greensboro because there was a studio there that he could record out of, but by this time school had started and I wasn't enrolled. Luckily while I was in Greensboro, I was able to run into Walter T. Johnson's mother, Yvonne Johnson who the same year President Obama became the first black President, she had become the first black mayor of Greensboro. At the time, she was about to run for City Council at Large and asked me to intern with her while I was in Greensboro.

Ironically enough, my brother and I had a falling out about something and I found myself out of school and stuck in Greensboro for the first time in years for no reason... or so I thought. But at that moment I was car-less, homeless, and jobless; which was not the plan or my train of thought when I left school after making a 3.7 for the semester!

Chapter Ten: *Still Dreamin*

Dwellin' on the past when you were alright
When you were getting cash but wasn't too bright
Now your luck down, you feel like bustin' them shells
Nobody owes you, can't do anything for self
Want niggas to show you, how to come up with green
I schemed since I'm 14, what the f%k was your dream?*

-Nas (Still Dreamin')

I would go to Mrs. Johnson office and sit and talk with her. For all I remembered, she was the cat lady. When I was younger, my dad would take me to her house, and I called her the cat lady because she would have so many cats on our porch. I mean like 10 to 15 at a time. She and my father had a genuine friendship. I could tell by the passion in her voice when she spoke about it. For the longest time, it had been taboo to admit that I was Rev. King's son.

I didn't have to when I was in Durham but I was back in Greensboro, and I fell right back into what I ran from. The crazy thing was that people did not react the way I thought they would when they found out who I was. I thought they would be judgmental, but they weren't. They were excited to see me and they all loved to tell me their favorite Rev. King story. I think it was important to Mrs. Johnson that she dispelled a lot of what I thought about my father. I was young when I lost him and according to the media, he was the scum of earth... at least that's how I interpreted.

When I was in college, sometimes I would Google my father's name and the only thing I could find was all the negative articles that were written about him. I couldn't find articles on how he had employed hundreds of people, provided housing for hundreds of families, or even that he made the City of Greensboro money that they are still counting today from property taxes. What I could find was, "he stole this, and he did that." But Mrs. Johnson made sure that I understood the entire story, and she changed my life during that internship. It was almost like when Simba ran into Rafiki in the jungle, and Rafiki had to remind Simba who he was. Mrs. Johnson was my Rafiki.

Mrs. Johnson encouraged me to start a nonprofit and to continue to do community development work like my father did. At that time I knew that I had more social capital than most 22-year-olds my age. So I embraced my newly found purpose for my life and that was centered around community development. It also meant that I would have to do something that I promised myself I wouldn't do, and that was to move back to Greensboro.

At the time I was staying with a brother who went to NC A&T named Greg Hill. Greg was my fraternity brother and was much like me in image and persona. He ran a company called JoinMe, and he did a lot of political activism on the campus. We grew a brotherhood quickly and in my time of uncertainty, he encouraged me and pushed me to think big and to not be afraid of greatness. I took him back to NCCU with me to attend that year's training day. He had him a nice comfy seat with our cheerleader team Champagne, and it felt nice to have exchanged a glimpse into each other's collegiate legacy.

I also meet a brother name DC who was a student at WSSU, much like me, he was a party host. I stayed between DC and Greg's place much of that fall semester. I was interning, and it was pretty hard. Money was hard to come by, but both of those brothers showed me a lot of love, and made sure I was as together as possible. DC took me to WSSU's homecoming that year and had me feeling like a celebrity. Both he and Greg had that persona that would give the impression that they knew everyone in the room, or at least everyone in the room knew them. It was funny to see my reflective self in both of those brothers.

I can almost remember hearing the conversation in my head that lead me to urban farming. I had met a talented brother named Derek who moved to Greensboro from Winston. We were hanging out one night, and he told me he could show me how to make a million dollars off of three acres of land. He then took me over to the computer and pulled up YouTube and typed in, "Will Allen," and then a light bulb went off.

Will Allen was born in Virginia on a farm and is a very large man. He went on to become one of the first black basketball players at the University of Miami. After graduation, he went overseas to play basketball where he encountered innovative ways of farming, and one of these methods was aquaponics. Aquaponics is a closed looped system that incorporates aquaculture and hydroponics to create both produce and protein in the same system. The fish waste is used as liquid nitrogen fertilizer to help the plants grow, and the plant waste filters out the water to help grow the fish. This is a very efficient way of growing food if done properly. Will Allen moved back to the United States and moved to Milwaukee and acquired the last 3 acres of zoned agriculture land, and that is where his organization Growing Power is located today. He is one of the largest food producing nonprofits in the Midwest.

Will Allen

Greg Hill

I was hooked. I couldn't learn enough about this system and about Mr. Allen. I started to conceptualize what the nonprofit could be and how it could be centered around food production. Then I learned about a term called food deserts and that Greensboro ranked in the top 5 nationally in food insecurity. It seems to be a perfect fit. The only thing I was missing at the time was knowledge.

I would travel with Derek and his group to Atlanta to throw twenty five and up parties at a place called Lucky's lounge. What I enjoyed most about this experience was that all of these parties were with celebrities, and the fact that I was not twenty five and technically was not supposed to be in the club. It would be a group of five or six of us that would travel down to Atlanta, and I was by far the youngest person in the group.

A guy named Red was the leader of the group, he was a middle aged gentlemen who carried himself well and ironically was always talking about industrial hemp. Red took care of the group and always made sure we stayed in really nice hotels and ate well. I was out of school at the time and had some spare time, so I would make the trip without thinking twice.

The first trip was an after party for the BET awards

show that was hosted by Cedric the Entertainer, and I was really excited to meet him. At the party the thing that stood out the most about being around Cedric the Entertainer was this other gentlemen with him in a black jacket who looked just like Red Foxx. Near the end of the party I was able to get my picture taken with him and exchanged a few jabs back and forth after he found out I was an Alpha. He claimed he was being set up. (Laugh out Loud)

Cedric the Entertainer

After that party we were called back down about two weeks later to do a Slick Rick party, and personally I have yet to see anyone in my life wear as much jewelry as I saw Slick Rick had on that night. That was a dope party as well, and I think a lot of people got a kick out of me knowing the words to Slick Rick, but I was in there jamming! After the party on the way back to North Carolina, I remember Red saying that the next party was going to be a big one and I remember thinking, 'I wonder who they are planning on bringing!' It would be about a another two or three weeks before we would head back to what would be the most memorable party I've ever been a part of. So, we get the call to head down.

Red had left for Atlanta a few days earlier to make sure that everything was smooth, but I was still unclear who was coming to this party. Probably by the time we got to South Carolina Derek obviously couldn't keep it to himself and told me, "Hey look man we headed to do this party with Mary J. Blige." My mouth dropped, I had to gather my thoughts before I responded to him, but it seemed as if the only words I could manage to say was, "okay." My dad use to always tell me no

126

matter how excited you are at that moment, always act as if you have been there before, so I did. But on the inside I was beyond excited.

The closer we got to Atlanta we were able to pick up their radio stations and Mary J was on the air, and that's when everything became real to me (laugh out loud). Keith Sweat had called up to the radio station to welcome her to the city and at the end of the interview she says, "And tonight I am going to be at Lucky's Lounge." Bingo! The party was on and I knew that our party was the place to be that night. After checking in the hotel and grabbing some food, we headed to the club to set up early as we always did. This time we had Hennessy waiting on us with promo material since they were helping sponsor the party that night. They had some lime green shades with their logo on the side that I grabbed and put on my face (this will be important later on in the story, pay attention).

Well obviously, all of Atlanta was in attendance because the line was wrapped around the building. I remember going back and forth outside hoping to see her pull up, and to show people in line that this young guy had the ability to go in and out as he pleased (so vain shaking my head). After a few failed attempts, I finally timed my exit perfectly to witness her pull up to the club, and it was certainly a sight to see.

It reminded me of the cartoon wacky racers. There was a character on the cartoon called Penelope Pitstop who drove a pink dolled up car. Except, Mary was in a pink dolled up Bugatti with two black SUV's to the front and the back of her. This will go down in my book as the most boss way to pull up at your own event ever.

Once she got in and settled on stage, the party really got jumping, and she was even surprised by Monica Brown showing up to the party. I remember walking with my VIP pass into the VIP section thinking I don't have five dollars in my pocket right now, but I am right next to Mary J and Monica, this is crazy. But not as crazy as it would get because about an hour into her being at the club another guest decided to show up and surprise her, Young Jeezy. Now I have personally been a Snowman fan since boyz n the hood, and can even remember being in Memphis when the song with him and Mannie Fresh came out, that was my anthem for the summer.

The club is at a fever pitch when the DJ announced that Young Jeezy had just walked him, and to my amazement he only walked in the club with him and one other partner, who looked more like a friend than he did his security. If I ever run into Young Jeezy, I can get him to remember this night because once him and his partner walked into VIP I had my lime green Hennessy shades on literally a few feet away from him. And our protocol at the party was once everything was taken care of you could enjoy yourself. So, I am sure as he looked at me confused he was wondering what the heck my young self was doing in the VIP section, but in my defense I was working. I certainly gave him a head nod to say what's up, but I guess he was feeling more confused than friendly at the moment.

But the next few moments burned in my memory forever. The DJ stopped the music and said that Young Jeezy, who had an album coming in a few months (TM103), had an exclusive never before heard song he wanted to debut for Mary J. Now I don't know if it was the first time he had ever played it in public, but I am for certain that was the first time I had ever heard the song. So, as I am less than five feet away from Young Jeezy, the song starts out with a really slow melody with him saying, "Hey Cherie we in here, 5 o'clock in the morning.. it might be 3 though." And the baseline dropped, "I see some ladies in here I might marry," and the entire club went crazy. I looked to my left, and I saw Mary J and Monica dancing and I looked to my right and saw the entire club jamming out to what would be his hit single "I do," featuring Jay- Z and Andre 3 Stacks.

I think the thing that was coolest about the situation was how cool Young Jeezy was to see the crowd reaction. He acted just as if he had been there before. And I took note. We did one last party in Greensboro with DJ Drama that turned out to be an amazing party, but ended in the worst way possible with money being stolen. During the party DJ Drama's manager Pat was mad cool, and it was a good experience seeing that side of the music industry, the side I thought I was going to be able to see with my brother.

Pat was the person I had set out to become when I initially left college. But by the end of the night the taste of throwing parties and being a music mogul completely left my mouth, and I knew it was time for a change I had thrown parties before but that isn't the same as running a business, especially not one as sophisticated as an operational nonprofit. The one thing I did know was how my dad operated, so I went knocking on doors looking for support. The next semester I went back to Durham to finally finish undergrad and to start my new career. I no longer wanted to be a high school history teacher, a music mogul, or a party promoter. Now, I was going to be a successful social entrepreneur.

With the help of my friend from undergrad name Candi, I was able to file all of my proper paperwork to rename and rebrand my nonprofit. I will be forever grateful for her being in my life, and the belief she had in me early on my path. She once told me she had a dream about me getting into NCCU's Hall of Fame. I can't wait to see that happen, she'll be one of the first people I thank. Even with all the help that I would get from Candi, I was still way in over my head. Luckily for me God would step in and send an angel my way to set me on my path.

Eric had set up a meeting with a lady named Andrea Harris. She was the President of North Carolina Institute of Minority Economic Development and prior to me her, we heard that if we could get into her good graces, that life would be so much better. She has the reputation of being one of the most powerful business women in the state of North Carolina, and the day we met with her she immediately grabbed me and hugged me as if I was one of her children. She looked familiar to me, but I didn't really know who she was. She explained to me how she had helped my father get his start in the community development business along with her and another one of my angels, Mrs. Daphne Slogan Morgan. They helped my father take Project Homestead to heights no one could ever imagine it would reach.

At the time Eric and another friend of mine, Antonio Fuller, was helping me get the nonprofit started. She ended up offering all three of us internships after she realized none of us knew what we were talking about. They would have to build what Mrs. Morgan like to call our "business acumen," The first thing they wanted to expose us to was that successful minority businesses ran across the state. Then they exposed us to powerful political figures. They also showed us the basics of creating a business centered on making a business plan. I was rolling around with Ms. Harris and she made sure she exposed me to as much as she could and like Mrs. Johnson, I could tell how genuine her friendship with my father was by the passion in her voice when she spoke about him.

One of our first trips was to the North Carolina General Assembly, to learn more about state government and how it functions. There were some familiar faces there to greet me. Congresswoman Alma Adams was then a State Rep and my grandmother, Elaine Pamon was a State Senator. One day we walked into the office and Mrs. Briles Johnson, director of the Women's Business Center, which was a component of NCIMED called us into the office and asked us to attend a Durham City Council meeting on international export trading. We attended a session with the U.S. Commerce; federal and state officials were there.

The event was the televised version of what we sat through the prior week, and we were encouraged to participate if we could. I saw this as the perfect opportunity to get up and speak. I don't even remember what I said, but I said it. For the next few months random people would say hey I saw you on T.V. It was a first time experience but it certainly wouldn't be the last. Happenstance, it was the first time people began to notice my shift from just party promoter to businessman

One week we were preparing to host a guy name, Randal Pinkett. Prior to the awards dinner, that they invited him to come speak, but I have never heard of him. I read in a press release that he had just signed a contract with the government for over $900 million dollars, and immediately he became one of my favorite people. He had written a book called "Campus CEO" which he signed for me and that book became my bible in regards to starting my business.

The night he came to Raleigh to speak he was standing up giving his remarks and I remember looking around the room. It was filled with successful and powerful people and of course, Ms. Harris had me sitting in the front. Numerous times during the dinner I envisioned myself rising to the top just as he did. Ms. Harris and I made eye contact and had an unspoken conversation as if she was saying I expect you to be just as great as him.

Ms Harris and Michelle Gathers-Clark   Obba Babtunde

I grew up so much at my time at NCIMED. I learned so much and it took me to levels that I could never imagine I would reach. At the time I was in a relationship with this girl name India who is someone I will always cherish. I was no longer the Prince that NCCU had known. All of a sudden I began to have a strong desire to become Matthew again. The crazy thing is that when I came back to NCCU, I decided that I was done throwing parties and that I wanted to give my undivided attention to starting my business. I am sure that's not what India expected when we got together.

I was meeting people like Martin Ekes, President of Self Help and Abdul Rasheed, President of the North Carolina Community Development Initiative. I even met Bob Brown, who was a consultant for the Mandela estate. Ultra-powerful and successful people were coming into my life, and they kept telling me that I was on the right path and to keep going. They told me stories about how they knew my father, but I didn't have two pennies to rub together and that was the word around campus. Prince wasn't the same Prince. Little did they know that Matthew was finally coming to take his place. It was a bittersweet during that time because I had been so used to throwing parties to buffer my lifestyle, but I had to sacrifice that to start my business.

I once had a dream that I only spoke to my mother about. In this dream, I was walking into a gas station and I notice that the newspaper had my picture on the front page and when I picked it up the headline said, "Like father... Like Son." I could tell that it was a joyous article. It wasn't negative at all. When I woke up, I didn't know who I could tell, but I had to tell somebody. So I called my mother, and she didn't laugh, which is important to me when I share my dreams with someone. She just said that it's probably going to happen.

One day while at the office I got a phone call from Sheriff BJ Banes office in Greensboro. He was a close friend of my father and was always so nice to me as a child. While I was in Greensboro interning for Mrs. Johnson, he allowed me to join him on his weekly television show, and I am sure if you ask him he will tell you I was really nervous. He had called me to tell me a lady from the local newspaper wanted to do a story on me.

The same newspaper that had trashed my father's name now wanted to interview me. I told him that I was flattered but I would have to respectfully decline. When he asked why, I mentioned to him that I really didn't trust the media and I didn't want to put myself out there too much. He understood but encouraged me to think about it. What really triggered my interest about the matter was when he said the writer's name... Susan Ladd.

Chapter 11: *It Was All a Dream*

Then B.I. said, Hov remind you
Nobody built like you, you designed yourself
I agree I said, my one of a kind self
Get stoned every day like Jesus did
What he said, I said, has been said before
Just keep doing your thing he said, say no more

-Jay-Z (It Was All A Dream)

At that present moment, I could not remember why that name sounded so familiar to me. It wasn't until I got home that night that the light bulb went off in my head. I had a framed article that I kept in my room of my father back in 1995 and she was the same person who wrote the article. In that particular article, my father had just gotten Project Homestead up and running, and we had our church at our Ball Street location. It was right before my father hit the next levels of his professional career. So, that night I prayed about it and asked God to allow me to feel the answer in my spirit.

The next morning I woke up and was moved to try to get in contact with her. We set up a sit down meeting at NCIMED for the next week. For the time in years, I was a nervous wreck in regards to what she wanted from me. Was she setting me up like they did my father? I didn't know, so I consulted with Ms. Harris. I told her that this lady from the newspaper wants to do a story on me but I didn't know about what. Ms. Harris told me to pray about it and that if I didn't feel comfortable at any point during the interview to stop and come get her (laugh out loud).

Ms. Harris always had this protective motherly spirit about her when it came to me, and everyone in the office knew it. It's funny because I know God has a sense of humor, and if you ask him for something he will make it happen in his own creative way. The next week we met as planned and for some odd reason, Mrs. Ladd's spirit drew me to her. I can't really put into words why I drew to her... but I just felt as if I could trust her. God gave me a sense of calmness that I had not felt in a while and at that point, the only thing I wanted to do is to tell our side of the story; the story that was not printed–the story I couldn't find on Google.

I wanted her to know the damage those articles had done to me and my family, and I wanted her to know how hard life had been since my father passed away. I wanted her to know that I felt as if certain people in the city had torn my family apart and that it took me awhile to get past that. With Mrs. Johnson help, of course, but it was one point during our interview I could see her getting teary eyed. I didn't know if journalist were allowed to have emotions. My experience with the media personnel had painted a picture of them being cruel and heartless, but she tore that wall down.

I spoke about the resentment that I held in my heart for my father for so long. I was young and didn't understand the entire story. I was only able to piece the story together based off of what everyone told me. I talked about how it became taboo for me to admit that I was his son especially after the gay allegations came out. But in my mind, my father left me believe those allegations. For the longest time, I was so frustrated with him. I felt as if I was dealing with life situations that I would not have dealt with if he was still alive.

I had a buddy in college name Corey and his history was much like mine. He was the son of a successful businessman and Corey was in college with the benefits from the success of his dad. Corey was a really good guy; and I never was jealous of him directly, but I always wondered how my college experience would have been like if my father was still around. I certainly would not have had financial issues, and I probably would have never joined the military. At the same time, those experiences helped shape my character. So even in my sorrow; I found a bright spot in the story.

And then she did something that blew my mind–she apologized for her involvement in the articles that caused me so much pain. She said she didn't write them, but she did nothing to stop them either. I mention to her the guy's name who wrote those articles and how I would never forget him. As a child of God, I was required to forgive him, but I would never forget. I expressed to her that even if everything they said about my father was true; it still should not demonize him to the point to where nothing else he accomplished in his life mattered especially once he died. After he died, it was like they went into overdrive to tarnish his legacy and he wasn't here to defend himself. They were just being very vindictive.

It wasn't fair that he had sacrificed so much for so many individuals, and that his legacy was not even recognized. There were countless families that would have never experienced homeownership if it wasn't for Michael King. I was a child at the time, so I wasn't trying to justify or defend what had happened within the organization because I didn't know; neither did I make any decisions. Michael King was a good person, and he was one hell of a father. That's really the only thing I wanted to express.

During the interview, Ms. Harris came down into the room to check on me as she said, but it was a quick check to make sure Mrs. Ladd was doing right by me... and she was. Ms. Harris talked about her position of being able to see both my father and I get our start in community development work and that she saw a lot of similar traits we shared. Mrs. Ladd finished the interview, and I thanked her for reaching out to me. She told me the next week a photographer would be coming to take my picture.

When the guy came to take my picture, we had a tough time figuring out what kind of shot he wanted to take. That is until I took my jacket off and he saw the tattoo on my arm. He asked to see what it was, and I showed him the Lion I got for my father and he took a picture of it. The next week while I was still living in Durham, people were blowing my phone up to tell me not only did I make the paper, I was on the front page—yeah, God has a sense of humor alright.

I didn't know Mrs. Ladd was going to do this, so I called Mrs. Johnson and then Mayor Robbie Perkins to add comments to the article. Mr. Robbie had been my buddy since my childhood. He and my father were friends and I could tell that he came from different perspectives when it came to life, but they found common ground and built a friendship with my dad. I remember Mr. Robbie use to give me Duke Basketball tickets every year for my birthday. He graduated from Duke and he knew I was a huge Duke fan.

The article was published the Sunday before the 2012 presidential elections. My mom called me and read the article aloud to me since I didn't have access to it at that moment. One thing I did have access to were the comments posted about the article online and many of them were less than flattering. If I had thought that all the animosity for my father had left with him then I could think again because those comments slapped me back to reality real fast. Some of the comments questioned whether or not I would be stealing taxpayers' money like my father.

Other comments asked if I would be building houses with swimming pools based off of my nonprofit. Some of the comments were just downright ugly. I mean these people didn't know me from Adam, but they were not pleased with what was on the front page of the newspaper. The comments had me wondering, "Am I wrong to want more for my life? Should I not get compensated for the sleepless nights it took me to put all of this stuff together?" And more importantly, "could I take the heat of knowing that there would be people who would be against anything I did no matter my reason or purpose?"

I credit my Pastor Corey Graves for keeping my balance and focus. He always reminds me that what I was doing was for the Glory of God and not for the pleasure of man. He reminded me that people would have opinions regardless of the facts and to keep my head into what got me on the front page of the paper and to not look back. Those conversations were only affirmations to what I had said to myself earlier. I made a pact with myself that I wouldn't succumb to the same nonsense and foolishness that hampered my father. To be frank, I had gotten to the point where I acknowledge that nobody who left a nasty comment on that page paid any of my bills or student loans. They didn't even give me a shoulder to cry on. From that day forward they would no longer be in control of my happiness.

The week after that Ms. Harris sent me to one particular conference in Greensboro that was hosted by the Support Center and I ran into a buddy of mine name, Reggie Delaney who works for the City of Greensboro. He introduced me to Dr. Mark Smith who worked for the Guilford County Health Department and who wrote the disparity study on food deserts in Guilford County. All of a sudden my vision was starting to come around full circle.

I began to work with Dr. Smith on understanding the issue of food deserts from his perspective. Dr. Smith was familiar with Will Allen and understood how he used aquaponics as a means for community development. Dr. Smith provided me with maps of the food desert areas in Guilford County, and I was able to start to conceptualize the problem from his perspective. There were no grocery stores within miles of these communities, and this became the direct effect on the chronic health disparities that plagued those communities.

Dr. Smith brought me to a church that he said had donated 3 acres of land to the health department to do an agriculture project on. The church was called Prince of Peace Lutheran Church. This church had started a community garden and ran a curbside market for the past three years prior to my arrival. I loved the spirit of the congregation. They genuinely wanted to make a difference for their community and under Pastor Tim's leadership; they started making that change. It was there I met Ms. Niesha Douglas and Ms. Marianne Legreco. Both of these ladies have enhanced my experience tremendously with their passion and commitment to finding a solution for this problem.

My work wasn't about helping people become first time low-income homeowners, and that's what I loved about it. It was my very own mission that I could peruse while honoring my father. The final semester of undergrad for me was all in preparation for moving back to Greensboro. I thank Dr. Jim Harper and Dr. Rhonda Jones for guiding me through my undergrad experience and encouraging me to follow my dreams back to Greensboro. Dr. Jones even agreed to come work for my nonprofit once I got things going. That final semester, my then girlfriend who was the captain of the cheerleading team had broken up with me TWICE in the same semester and finally for good. She moved in with Eric and one of our older frat brothers Tyronne James (now known as Baba Gdey Dogon). Ty had been one of the pillars of our chapter and is credited to have helped mastermind the development of the new brand of Gamma Beta.

I appreciated the environment in which I was able to flourish under. Both of them were in their Master of Arts program(s) which gave me a lot of inspiration to finish my undergraduate career. I guess it's one of those iron sharpens iron type of things, but I always enjoyed being the little brother in the group. My last semester, I was able to enjoy that brotherhood and all its ups and downs. Tyronne helped me complete my 501(c) 3 non-exempt application for my nonprofit, and he should be credited with bringing a lot of legitimizing to my organization. We had many late night conversations that semester about life and its purpose. He even helped me get over my then girlfriend. I never had my heart broken by a woman before, so that was a difficult time for me.

Ty encouraged me to stay focused on graduating and to strive towards taking my business to the next level. I appreciated his psychology based background that was centered in Afro-thought; he helps expand my mind. It was starting to sink in that this chapter of my life was actually closing as I reflected on my experience in Gamma Beta chapter of Alpha Phi Alpha. The brotherhood had become my family. I was never the type that wanted what I was associated with to define me but that's what I love about Gamma Beta. They allowed me to be me while still making me a better man. I love my set–the 68th House of Alpha Phi Alpha made me into a man and set the standard of achievement so high. I cherish all of my Gamma Beta brothers. "GB… GB… Yeah my brother, GB!"

Chapter 12: *Good Morning*

But you graduate when you make it up outta the streets
From the moments of pain, look how far we were done came
Haters saying you changed, now you doing your thang

-Kanye West (Good Morning)

The day of my graduation I had a very surreal feeling. It was much different from my high school graduation because it was understood that I would graduate high school, but college wasn't promised, I left college twice. Thank God I found my way back and finished the journey. That morning I had Kanye's Graduation album on repeat which I thought was fitting because it was released my freshman year in college. As for any big event in my life, and in the back of my mind, I knew that my father wouldn't be there physically and I can almost always predict that I will have to take some time to myself.

As my mother once said, "there is no time he absence from us. He might as well died yesterday as far as we are concerned," but like Tupac once said, "Life Goes On." I had so many mixed feelings that day. I was excited, I was nervous, I was sad, and I was numb—my undergrad career was coming to an end. The place that took a lost boy from Greensboro and turned him into a man with purpose would soon become a memory. Even after all that I have accomplished in my career, me not being becoming Mr. NCCU will probably always haunted me. It was expected of me since my freshman year. I just felt like I let myself down. Nevertheless, my experience at North Carolina Central University was so dynamic that I am proud to admit my desire to become one of its most influential graduates. I love my HBCU.

The Crew

Gamma Beta on MLK Day

Funny enough I thought I was going to feel some type

of way towards my mother the day of my graduation. In my mind, I always knew how I really felt but these thoughts could never be formulated into words. These thoughts and feelings stemmed from pain; the pain of knowing that my mom had no idea of the man I had become. When she saw me walk across the stage, I knew she had no clue of who I had become.

But all in all, that day I was just happy to have her there. I felt so proud to see her face every time someone came up to her and hugged her on my behalf as if they knew her their entire life. That is the type of love NCCU provided me. It was the love she couldn't provide me or maybe forgot how to. That night I had thrown my last party with Harper as "EnvyUS." It was a fitting way to end an era, and I felt like I owed it to our friendship to at least cherish that moment of graduating together and finishing what we had started. I mean that's just the type of guy I am. I am loyal to those who are loyal to me, and he brought me into his family. If I wasn't in Memphis for the holidays I was at his house, but what he couldn't see was that my foot was already one foot outside of the friendship ready to close the door.

One day two years prior, I was preparing to take a trip to App State for a football game we had against them. Before we left, I was lying in bed that morning. I was woken up by Malachi who was calling me on three way from jail. He was upset, to say the least. I had to calm him down and ask him what was going on, and all I could make out initially was "I am going to kill Harper." The first thing that came to mind is like—whoa brother, you not even home yet and you talking about going back already? I asked him to slow down and tell me what happened. He goes on to tell me how he found out that Harper was talking to Beth.

It was the grace of God that required me to go to that game that day, and that game forced us to travel a few hours away from Durham. There is no telling what I would have done if I was allowed to skip out on the game, which I asked to do, but by the grace of God and my line brother Dwayne, they both were able to at least talk the anger out of me while we were on the bus. Dismissing all of my options as solutions, assuring me I had more to lose by choosing any of what I was suggesting to do, I took a step back and regrouped. After the anger was gone, I just felt hurt.

I gave my sister way more of a pass than Harper, who was a year older than me. My sister being wide eyed by college boys, did what most younger girl siblings would do given the opportunity–she talked to one of older brother siblings friends. I still saw this as an opportunity to show her the lesson. I mean, after all, she was my little sister. I already don't bring much family to the table and Harper knew that. Shortly after speaking to my sister about their involvement with each other, Harper text me confessing his secret love for my sister and that he was going to tell me, but he didn't know how or that I knew. It was bullshit because he was the same guy I was with all the time, so to see him intentionally play my sister was a cup of karma that I was not ready for.

I didn't talk to him for weeks. I avoided his calls until I could process what it meant for me. I never brought the situation up even when we started talking again. I felt that as a man I shouldn't have to. It was his situation to talk about but he never did. I should have taken that as a sign. I just thought in my mind when I leave Durham, I am leaving this friendship with it. That feeling only intensified for me as our college career played out. In many aspects he was the top Kappa, and I was the top Alpha. Although it was only campus wide, I understood the politics at all levels and any public rife between him and I would have undone all the divine nine unity we had worked to build on campus.

Initially, I wanted to put my hands on him but I had too much love for his family to do that. I mean I was a pallbearer in his grandfather's funeral. When his girlfriend passed away freshman year in a car accident, I was the one with him the next morning helping him get through that. At any rate, the EnvyUs party would be my last involvement with Harper although I got nothing but love for what our friendship provided. In my mind, it would also be the end of "Prince," at least for time being. I was very satisfied with life that day. I didn't take for granted that most people didn't even get to experience college moreover get a chance to graduate.

I understood that a lot of people who started college with me didn't get to cross that stage for one circumstance or another, but God had granted me favor beyond my faults to experience obtaining my degree. I was satisfied but not content. It was time to go back to Greensboro, and I was ready, or at least I thought I was. I had been accepted into NC A&T graduate program to get my Master of Science degree in Agriculture Education and was excited to further my education. When I got home, it hit me to why I spent so much time away from home especially when trying to pursue my education. Just being in Greensboro was a distraction in itself. I was not quite prepared for it.

Chapter 13: *Return of Simba*

So this is who I speak fo'
To give the young niggas somethin' they could reach fo'
You better dream, boy

-J.Cole (Return of Simba)

I moved back to Greensboro in the summer of 2013, and it was just like Simba returning to Pride Rock just to find that Scare had destroyed everything. The biggest difference between this time and the time I was interning for Mrs. Johnson was during my internship I was still flying under the radar. I was still in and out the city for those few months and rarely went past places I didn't have to see.. i.e. my dad's church or anything that reminded me of my childhood for that matter. Now that I was back there was no escaping it, not only did that newspaper article made me recognizable it set forth major expectations for me. In all actuality, I didn't know what the people expected from me. I wasn't in Greensboro when the article came out so for the most part when people saw me that was the first time they had seen me in 7 plus years.

Before I left for college things were holding on by a thread in regards to what I recognized from my former life. My dad's church was still intact for the most part. Although I could see the writings on the wall, the church wasn't the same. Growing up I didn't have much biological family around me. My mom's entire family was still in Memphis and Chicago. My father didn't have as much blood family as she did so the church was my family.

For the first time, I was able to gauge the magnitude of my father's death as it related to everyone else. Marriages that I would never suspect to break up broke up. People who were employed by Project Homestead in one way or another were now struggling to pay bills, and my father's church had become a shell of itself. I attended service one Sunday, and it was like someone was playing a bad joke on me. What once was a great village with 500 plus membership had broken into 4 new churches and scaled down to fewer than 40 people.

When people saw me, I could see a small ray of hope in their eyes and without saying it, I could tell they wanted my father back. They were not directly asking me to be my father, but I could hear the optimism in their voice when they learned that I had moved back to town. It was a heavy burden to carry around because everywhere I looked my father's work was evident. In areas that use to be lively and vibrant, now laid dormant, and I was determined to find some answers.

One night I was downtown Greensboro at this popular spot called the "Snack Bar." I enjoyed the food there, and the owner was pretty cool. That night I had placed an order for pickup and while I was waiting for my food, I started to engage in a conversation with a gentleman and another lady. I knew the gentleman, but I have never seen the lady before. Somehow the owner made a reference to my father and the gentleman and I spoke about my dad for a few minutes, and then his order came up and he left

My order was ready and as I was putting my napkins in my bag the lady came up to me with a very soft voice and said, "Excuse me, did they say you were Rev. King's, Son, Michael King?" I said, "Yes ma'am," and immediately her facial expressions changed. She looked at me for a second and then she said, "Your dad was a great man. I just remember the city being so sad when he passed. It was like a dark cloud was over the city right after died." I stood there blank for a moment. Then I thanked her for her kind words and I departed.

On my ride back home, I thought about something. Had I ever took into consideration the outside perception of my father's death? Why did that lady's words hit me so hard? Had I let the media shape my perception of how I thought the city felt about my dad? I was presented an opportunity to rejoin Mrs. Johnson's campaign team again. Two years had passed, and it was election season. I was also presented with an opportunity to intern with the Mayor Robbie Perkins.

I didn't really think much of it when I was offered. I just moved back to the city and like I said earlier, Mr. Robbie had always been generous to me, so I didn't mind helping him out. I was to shadow him around the city and help leverage relationships for him with young voters.

Contrariwise, I did not know that he was dealing with some personal issues at the time. I enjoyed the time I spent with him and he taught me a lot—especially about life. He was able to keep a positive attitude about his situation although I felt as if people were treating him unfairly. I was always the type to just carry the understanding that we all struggle with something. Even public figures struggle and just because they are public figures, they are susceptible to criticism. I always wondered if those writing the stories had skeletons in their closets and if anything came out, how much mercy would they be looking for? As I reflect on the experience, my first interaction with some of Greensboro biggest power players was through my relationship with Mr. Robbie. In the long run he was the key to my reintroduction into the city.

I had also met a very special lady during my time in grad school. I had met her through my cousin's girlfriend, and she made a major impact on me. Unfortunately she had to move back to Maryland early in our relationship. Although we tried the relationship with each other, it did not survive the distance. I still credit her for a lot of my growth during this time. She and my cousin's girlfriend who ended up becoming family herself had a major influence on my maturing. I thank her for putting up with me when I moved back, and all the chicken dip she has provided over the years. I love your bones Kelisha.

my daughter and Mayor Perkins

I came up with a concept called the "City Oasis Project," and brought it to Dr. Smith for his approval. Dr. Smith helped me formulate the idea further; and soon thereafter, I was sitting back down in front of Mrs. Ladd showing her the property at the Prince of Peace church and giving her the details about the City Oasis Project. Once again we ended up back on the front page of the newspaper. This time I was in Greensboro for it and although I was humbled by the experience, I did not recognize its totality; it was a gift and a curse.

As a graduate student at NC A&T, it gave the school some good exposure, and I wanted nothing more than to be perceived at the "perfect graduate student," but my focus was all over the place. But as the saying goes, "it's always darkest before dawn." During my first year back in Greensboro, for some reason I was facing adversity back to back. Mr. Robbie lost his election, my brother had gotten locked up again, Derek had passed away the morning of one of my final exams, my grandmother's health was declining, and worst of all my daughter Faith, who lives with sickle cell, started experiencing frequent crisis's. Even my online classes were a hassle; those classes were hard. I was juggling a lot.

Long story short, I didn't finish the semester as well as I wanted to and the week after school let out, my grandmother passed away. That was the pinnacle of my first year back in Greensboro. "Nobody told me… the road would be easy." I had to endure so many trials and a tribulation that I was just left bare. I had to take an earnest look into the mirror and ask myself, "What are you going to do with your life cause it's kicking your ass?"

Figuratively, I wipe the blood off my nose and decided to walk upright with my head held high; I pushed forward. My grandmother's passing help start a much needed healing process for our family. The night after she passed away, we met up at our Uncle Ray's house. He had gathered much of my grandmother's things and there were pictures that he wanted us to see and have. After he brought out two big binders of pictures my mom, sister, brother, and I looked through the pile and got excited by each passing picture. We saw pictures of my father growing up, my grandfather in the military, and my grandmother while she was in college. We were able to see our parents and grandparents as people living their lives, and I could appreciate them as people.

My grandmother had a picture of my Uncle Edward and her brother. I had never met him but he had green eyes too. Grandma uses to say that I looked like him. We found some early articles on my dad. One article was written about him when he was just 20 years old and talked about how his church was a miracle. Then I saw a news article talking about how my father had honored two Mayors for their work in low-incoming housing. The two articles beside each other painted a poetic path of how my father started and how he transformed his life. I got to see the importance of understanding the legacy from which you come and this ultimately put purpose into my life. I was then able to better process my father as a man and just a man. He had good habits and bad habits. He did good things and bad things. He succeeded and failed but yet in still, my father was just a man.

The day after my grandmother's home going service my family decided to go to the zoo while my Uncle Billy and his family were in town from California. The surprising twist to the story was the fact that my mother wanted to come too. My mom and my dad's brother were known to have beef, and it had been so since my father passed away. We never had "family time" anymore and we never really discussed all that had to happen or even spent time together just to mourn.

When we all got together at IHOP that morning it was like our family therapy session had begun. Our table arrangement matched my uncles' personalities–totally opposites. My Uncle Ray and Uncle Billy sat diagonally from each other with their nephews sitting next to them. Each uncle tried to convince their nephew to change their lifestyle. Uncle Ray was trying to get Billy Jr to become a vegetarian while Uncle Billy was showing Ray Jr all the different types of meals that came with Pork. Jokingly, he called our table the "Bacon Club."

After we broke bread together, we all headed down to

the zoo. It was the first time since my father's funeral that we had all been in one location. The first cousins always had this bond between us. Growing up I remember spending time at uncle Ray's house and playing Nintendo games with Ray Jr. He was a few years older than me, but that was my buddy. My cousin Kiev has always been my baby because she was the only other girl in the family and she has grown to become such a beautiful woman. My cousin Billy Jr is a genius, and I don't use that word loosely. I'm excited to see what his future holds for him. But for that one day, The King family was back together; and although he wasn't physically there, we could all feel my father's presence and my grandparent's presence too.

Margett's Grandkids

After a long day of goofing off at the zoo, it finally hit me and I had to fight back the tears; I really missed my dad. It didn't help that my Uncle Billy looked so much like him either. I didn't really grow up around Uncle Billy because he lived in California. The times we did spent together we always had fun though. I understood that he was the jokester out of the brothers. I remember my dad having me call him when I was younger and him having a radio ad sounding voicemail with him being a big time DJ. It made me laugh. All the brothers favored each other, but it is almost scary how much my Uncle Billy reminded me of my dad. Out of the three, Uncle Billy was the easy going one and was serious about enjoying life.

I just remember that my mom kept saying how glad she was that she came on the trip and for all of us, it was a family time of reflection. More importantly; however, it was a time for healing. At the end of the day, you only have one family. We were able to enjoy each other's company without sorrow or pain. It was just joy, pure joy! It was a sign from God; almost like sending the dove with the olive branch. That day symbolized a sign of peace...it had been since December 6, 2003, since our family had last known real peace.

That summer also marked the start of my for-profit company called, Triad Food Hub. Triad Food Hub is a company that connects local farmers to local retail demand. It is a concept that came to me as I was doing an assignment for graduate school during that semester for Dr. Alston. I spoke about the lack of connectivity between local producers and local retail demand. My research lead me to understand that a food hub would be a great way to bridge the gap, and that it would become a great resource for both the producer and the consumer. I considered this my "Facebook" idea

During that summer, I spoke on a panel at Elon's Law School about food deserts in Greensboro. I was invited to speak at the event by Mrs. Kathy Elliott, who at the time was working for an organization called, Action Greensboro. At the conclusion of that event, she told me about a Shark Tank pitch competition that was coming to the area and thought it would be a good idea for me to participate in. At the time I only had conceptualized my nonprofit where it was ready to be pitched, so I really didn't give serious thought to it initially when she mentioned it to me.

Afterward, my mother and I left to head to Memphis to see our family, and it was just the two of us. I was really blissful about the fact that she had come to see me speak on the panel. I took the time to acknowledge her because I really wanted her to know how grateful I was for her support. We took the bus, and it was a trip her and I took regularly separate but we both took many times.

She and I both share introvert characteristics that make it easier for us to be around each other; I had my headphones on and she was reading her book. The mere fact that we were able to get our relationship back on track was a great feat. It was a very satisfying feeling. I always enjoyed going back to Memphis. It shaped a lot of my adolescence when my mother sent me up there for the summer after my dad passed away. It's a family full of women and I was the only teenage boy living near most of my aunts at the time. So anytime I was around all the attention was on me. Even with that, I never took advantage, but it was a welcoming feeling to connect with my support system in Tennessee.

I love all my aunts dearly, but my auntie Laura is my favorite. Auntie Laura and I have a very special bond. Her motherly touch towards me is what I think was missing from my mom. My Aunt Gwen is the fun aunt and has always been. I can remember as kids, she took Bethany and me to carnivals and to the Peabody Hotel to meet Shane Battier when the Grizzlies moved from Vancouver to Memphis. Everyone knows that I am the biggest Duke Basketball fan ever.

My Cousin Rhonda stills stay in our grandmother's house on Radford Road. She is a NASA researcher, and yes you read that correctly, there is a NASA researcher that STILL stays in the hood. I get a kick out of that every time I think about it. I always raid her book collection. She is one of the most brilliant people I know and is so modest about it. My cousin Junior is my ace boon coon. He is probably about 15 or so years older than me, but we are one of the few men on this side of the family so we naturally click.

During this particular trip though my Aunt Shell came to pick us up. My aunt Shell is my mom's only sibling, and she has the sweetest spirit. My aunt Shell stays past Olive Branch Mississippi in a location that you would not want to get lost in once the sun went down. Her and my Uncle Rommel had a nice house with a pool in the back and every country home amenity you could think of. We always joked about how there would be a house full of food and still my Aunt Shell would go to the store to get more just for us. It never bothered me though. I felt so good to be around my family. We stayed a few days as always and then headed back to North Carolina.

Chapter 14: *Sky is the Limit*

While we out here, say the Hustlers Prayer
If the game shakes me or breaks me
I hope it makes me a better man, take a better stand
Put money in my mom's hand
Get my daughter this college grant
So she doesn't need any man
Stay far from timid, only make moves when your heart's in it
And live the phrase "Sky's the limit"

-Notorious B.I.G (Sky's the Limit)

Memphis Family R.I.P Uncle Billy

On my way back on the bus, I looked up the Shark Tank competition and thought to myself, "why not?" I got back to Greensboro and told my boy Brandon what I had planned to do and we connected with a former partner. He supposedly had connections to senior living facilities, and I already had connected with four farmers who were in the midst of creating a minority farmer Co-Op in Caswell County. Armed with at least a concept and an elevator pitch, I called one of my older fraternity brothers Winston and pitched my idea.

I had always looked up to Winston. He was only a few years older than me, but he had built his own company for himself that he had started in undergraduate school. He had a story similar to mine. The biggest difference that separated us was a few hundred thousand dollars. Winston was doing well for himself and was always willing to listen to my ideas and give me advice. I never asked him for money prior to this conversation, and he confessed to me that it meant a lot to him that I didn't because that's how most people come to him.

So within two days, I had introduced Brandon and Winston who didn't know each other although we all graduated from the same college, and with everybody on the same page, we drove down to Greenville, NC and was ready to take Shark Tank on full steam. Winston had a very nice GMC SUV we drove down in. It made me feel like the "come up" was obtainable. It was raining, and we were running about 30 minutes late, but Winston quickly made that time up on the road.

Once we got there, we parked and rushed to the door to see Shark Tank staff greet us with instructions. We walked into this vintage looking building where we were given a pink Stark Tank band and a number telling us the time we could come back in order to give our pitch. We probably had two hours of waiting time in between and I was extremely nervous. I think I was more nervous than anything because I really had not thought out the business model to the company just yet and there was no business plan at all.

It was just a graduate school project and a dream. To get past my nervousness, I began to introduce myself to other entrepreneurs there, and we all found commonality in our jitters. There were roughly around 500 companies that pitched that day. It was everything from jarred pickles to foldable placement mats that zipped into a lunch bag for kids; to a bicycle that required no pedaling at all. All of these companies were good but we notice our opportunity in the fact that most of these items were novelty items in niche markets. We were dealing with food and that is something everyone could relate to.

Once it was our turn to pitch we were brought up stairs to a bigger room with about twenty other competitors. A gentleman from Shark Tank stood up and welcomed us here to the pitch competition and begun explaining rules and expectations. I looked over my shoulder and notice a few Shark Tank cast members pointing in our direction. While I was outside, I made it my point to meet every last staff person there and pitch to them. I didn't know that majority of the people I pitched to were only volunteers. But as God would have it that was enough to get the attention of one of the producers from ABC to come over and talk to us.

At first I didn't realize she was a producer and was kind of past the point of pitching my idea to another entrepreneur in my same position so I didn't do the most energy filled pitch, but lucky by that time Brandon and Winston had heard me pitch it so many times that they had caught on to the narrative. I could tell the lady was impressed, and I finally asked her, "Well what do you think ma'am? And she replied,
"I am Christiane Gomez. I am a producer for ABC." Immediately my posture changed, and I was attentive to every word that came from her mouth. She instructed us to come find her after we got finished pitching our idea, and our eyes grew as big as quarters. As she walked away I remembered thinking to myself, "Did she just say what I thought she said?"

but I did not have time to dwell on what just happened because as soon as she was out of sight the guy in charge called our number and we got up and headed towards the room where everyone pitched their idea.

Walking towards the room you could feel the excitement bounce off the three of us. At the time we didn't know what to make of what she had said to us. All that I know was that our confidence had grown, or so I thought. As we walked into the room, it was four tables with one judge at each table. Unlike any other pitch event I have seen, we would have to focus on our judges as three other companies pitched their idea as well. Walking up to our judge, I noticed that she was a younger judge and asked for our applications as we walked up.

As she instructed us to begin, I started talking and for as many times as I said it in my head, my nerves would not allow it to translate into what I had dreamed of that moment to be. I started stumbling over my word. I had no flow explaining the concepts and instead of giving off the impressed looked, I looked like utter confusion. Luckily the idea sparked her interest so instead of her shooting us down, she simply asked for me to clarify what I was saying. It was at the time Winston and Brandon took the wheel and to be honest, I think it was their energy that carried the pitch over with her. As we were talking she was taking notes on Winston's application and by the time she finished, the page was filled with notes. As they were talking, I looked around to see if the other judges were taking as many notes, they weren't.

I turned back and hopped in the pitch trying to redeem myself and helped finished our presentation to her. She smiled and said that this was the only food brokerage company she ran across their entire time during the event and she wished us the best of luck. Walking out Brandon and Winston were not bouncing off the wall as I walked out dwelling in shame. Both of them assured me that we did a great job and not to take it to heart, but I was disappointed in myself. I felt as if I missed the game winning shot and that if we didn't make it to the next step, it was all my fault. I felt as though I failed them.

Lucky as soon as we walked out the room, the producer we had spoken to earlier left a message for us with another producer to be back in two hours and that we had made it to the next round and to be prepared to pitch our idea on camera! Immediately that personal burden I was carrying around was lifted. We all ran to the car as fast as we could to celebrate in private and once we got in the car, there were screams of joy and high fives going all around.

We ran to grab some lunch and discussed our plans to pitch on camera, but it was more like us killing time and nervousness prior to heading back. We had no idea what was in store for us. Our ideas for how to pitch our idea were far and wide. We joked about having bloopers and silly back-and-mantras about what we were going to say and who was going to say it. After we finished our cipher, we hopped back into the car and headed back to the competition location. When we arrived, we rushed to the entrance and back upstairs. Butterflies filled my stomach but my head was clear. I was ready to redeem myself.

Walking back into the same room we pitched in, the Stark Tank crew had flipped the setup of the room into a full blown television production site. We had lights, cameras, and makeup artists! The same guy who gave the instructions before welcomed us all back. By this point, there were only 7 or 8 businesses left in the competition. We were all assigned numbers, and of course, we were assigned last to go. We waited and watched each company get their makeup done and be mic'd up in order to do their pitch. The pitch this round lasted about 15 to 20 minutes and the emphasis were to be as camera friendly as possible while pitching your idea.

Camera friendly is what we were. I mean it got to a point during the day that Winston was jabbing at people and when they asked him what we did, he would ask them to guess. The craziest response we received was that we were an R&B singing group. No one had guessed that we were involved in agriculture and what was our niche to our pitch. By the way, we were dressed I couldn't blame anyone. I had on a shirt and tie, Brandon had on jeans and a hat, and Winston had on a button down.

We looked like a younger version of LSG. Our confidence level was astronomic after we got a feel for everyone's performance. We just kept saying, "Let's be ourselves." Once our time came, our number was called, and we all got up to get ready. The makeup lady was an older white lady, but she was super kind and was joking with me to take out some of the nervousness. I was telling her about the person who called us an R&B group. She ensured me if that was the case she would be the first person one to buy our CD. The producer lady Mrs. Gomez who initially approached us walked up and asked if we were ready, and we all did our ROC BOY salute handshake and walked towards the shooting area. The producer asked us to do the handshake again, and we did it a few more times.

Once we were in front of the screen, it was hot; I remember it being really hot. The lights were bright, and I just kept reminding myself that I had been on camera before but nothing to this extent. Once we were given the cue to start, I began to start and immediately felt that this time would be different from the first go around. My words were flowing better and as I kept talking, I felt my nervousness leave. By this time Brandon and Winston got into the act as well; we all had chemistry between our words as if we had been working on this pitch for years, and
then it happens.

As we were kicking ass and taking names, Winston was following up on my comment about the ability to grow food in greenhouses, and I began to reel off different fruits and vegetables that could be grown. He started with tomatoes, lettuce, strawberries, and PINEAPPLES. Immediately Brandon and I paused and side eyed Winston. For those who do not know, pineapples come from pineapple trees; and therefore, it is generally thought of as a non-greenhouse crop. We recovered quickly, and that ended up being the laugh of the night. Once we were done, we got the biggest applause out of all the presenters. We didn't know if it was initially because we did a good job or because we were finally done shooting. It was a little past midnight so everybody was exhausted. Afterward, everyone came up to us telling us how well we did.

Even Mrs. Gomez came up to us and asked how to learn the ROC BOY salute. she said she was going to go home and teach her daughter. After saying our goodbyes, everyone went their own way. I don't know how it feels to win an NBA championship but as far as that night is concerned nothing came close. There were screams of joy, chest bumps, ROC BOY salutes; we even stopped the car a few times to dance in the street. That night was a special one, and we all knew it. It was something that we would remember for the rest of our lives.

The next day I was driving to see a family friend when Winston called me screaming to the top of his lungs. As I chuckled, I told him to calm down because I couldn't understand him. When we finally got his communication together, he told me that Mrs. Gomez had called him and told him that we made it to the next round. We were instructed to put together a video and then to head out to LA. I just remember looking at the phone like this cannot be real, but it was, and a 30 page application came along with it. Of course, instead of doing the responsible thing and filling out the application first and shoot the video second, we did it in reserve and it turned out to be a backward mishap.

I called my cousin Chris, and he agreed to shoot the video for us. But because we didn't have a warehouse, a truck or even a functional business, we decided to go to our community garden to shoot the video. Once we arrived everyone threw out their ideas on how our video should go. It was like a skit out of Mad TV. We all agreed that if Shark Tank didn't work out, we would send the bloopers to America's Funniest home videos. In shooting the video, we visited 3 farms and interviewed farmers to bring our concept more credibility and in all, it took us about 4 days to get the video completed. We had forgotten to complete our applications, and it was already Wednesday. Winston was out of town and we all had to turn in an application for each of us. Even worst, on Thursday morning Brandon called me to say that he reread the instructions and that the application had to be in California by Friday leaving us with a very short window to get this completed.

Without trying to be too frustrated we proceeded to explore every option there was to send our packages out but there were two issues. The first issue was that Winston was out of town and the second was that we didn't have the funds to send off the application using the express mail. For some reason that day we could not get in contact with Winston but had come across enough money to send the applications. So at this point, it had to be going on five or six o'clock that evening and we tried to the best of our ability to complete this 30 page application for each of us. The problem was that we didn't even have a business plan, more or less a 3 to 5 year financial track record, invoices, bank statements or anything.

Remember, our BIG IDEA was in its infantile stage. The application process had been overwhelming. The FedEx closed at nine and my Uncle Ray had agreed to pay the money needed to send off the applications; and then two more issues arose. First, I only had about five dollars' worth of gas in my car; and second, as soon as we were heading out the door it started raining very hard.

Winston and Brandon

On the way to the airport, Brandon and I tried to make light of the situation ensuring that we would look back on that night in a year from now and laugh about the obstacles that we were currently trying to overcome. We made it to the airport with about thirty minutes to spare, applications still incomplete. And even worse Winston's application hadn't even been started on. As we waited for my Uncle, we were desperately trying to finish the application in order for it to be sent off but it was not looking good. Brandon had sent an email to Mrs. Gomez explaining the situation, and she gave us a grace period of Saturday and that was perfect because we did not complete the application in time to send it off, anyway. On our way back from the airport Winston calls us back and we update him on what had happened. As the weather finally starts to clear up, I hear my engine start to rumble and five minutes away from our designation my car runs out of gas. At this point, I giggled to myself because I was thinking "whatever is waiting for me has to be great because I have been put through too many fires." Luckily, my homeboy, Omar was not far away and was able to come and take me to the gas station. Omar being a Morehouse man, he was always scheming about moves to make and encouraged us to do whatever we needed to do to get on Shark Tank, that was timely motivation. As we got situated Winston calls back and said: "pack your shit, you got a 8:05 am flight from RDU to LAX." At that very moment, the only thing going to my mind was the intro to B.I.G's "Going back to Cali."

By this time it was close to midnight, and I literally didn't have any cash to my name trying to get ready for a trip to LA. At the same time my cousin Chris and Kelisha, who I had been staying with, had moved out and as prideful as I was, I did not tell anyone that I was low-key homeless, except for Brandon. Brandon had been in the same boat as me, and we both were committed to seeing this venture change our lives for the better. Brandon at the time had a girlfriend who had moved away and had a few more days on the lease so I crashed there knowing that school would start back up soon and that my refund check would help me get another place.

Gathering my belongings for the trip, I decided to only take enough to fit into my book bag. My trip was only scheduled for a day, and I didn't have any money to live the LA lifestyle so my expectations were to just enjoy and observe. Brandon had given me his last thirteen dollars so that I would have enough gas money to make it to RDU airport and I was on my way. Arriving at the airport I should have tried to call somebody to leave my car with because I knew I didn't have money for the parking deck but at this point, I did not have a choice. It was going on four o'clock in the morning and I was dog tired. I got settled in the airport at my gate and checked in at the desk. As I was sitting there, all I could do was think about if my Dad was here right now—oh Lordy!

My flight that morning was pleasant. It had been a while since I had been on a plane but in my mind, I was laughing thinking about out of all the passengers on the plan, I had the least amount of money. I started talking to folk; everyone on my row wanted to know about Shark Tank. All the while, I was still working on completing the application. Once we landed, I was given many good wishes, and it made me feel kind of important; not that I was looking to be glorified, but it was just amazing feeling to see how far an idea had taken me.

After we landed I headed towards the exit. I only had my book bag, so I did not have to go to baggage claim. The issue that I was facing this time was that Winston didn't put the money in my account as promised, and all I was left with was three dollars out of the thirteen dollars Brandon had given me. On top of that my phone was about to die and Mrs. Gomez was not responding to any of my e-mails. In the meantime, my childhood friend Ish had moved to LA to do some work video shooting for a talent agency called CAA.

I called Ish and told him that I was in LA and he told me that if I took the bus near UCLA, he would meet me and take me back to his place. But of course, my phone dies. Not only does my phone die, but I only have the USB portion of the charger with no charger base to plug into the wall so, in order for me to charge my phone, I had to plug my laptop into the wall and plug my phone up that way. The issue with that is that there was an electrical shortage in my laptop portal so my phone would only charge to a point and then cut off. It would not charge past five percent so it continuously kept dying.

Finally, I had remembered that Mrs. Gomez had given me a number to call her on, and my phone stayed on long enough for her to tell me that she apologized that I made the effort but no one is allowed on set and that I could have just sent our package by mail, and she would not have been able to say that time would not have played a factor in their decision. She gave me an extension on Tuesday and also had me to contact two other people from ABC about my idea. They thought our video was very interesting, but they wanted to see our application. This put me in a very somber mood. Ironically, as soon as I hung up the phone with them my phone cut off and it took its sweet ole' time to turn back on. It took so much time that I just took a risk and caught the bus following

Ish's instructions hoping to lock down a place of refuge.

I said to myself, I would find a way to call him because staying at the airport was doing me no justice. Magically, my phone cut back on and I wrote down Ish's instructions on how to get near the WestSide of Hollywood where he lived. The weather was pleasant and standing still, but once I started walking my body heated up and that added to my growing frustrations. I walked down the street to what I thought was a bus stop. Luckily an older lady who obviously saw that I was not from the area and who could probably see my frustrations informed me that if that I walked a block over that a bus would come soon and that I would be able to ride that bus all over the city for a dollar. That immediately lifted a temporary burden for me as I didn't know how much the bus rides cost. I had flown across the country and did not even have enough money to take a bus around the city.

After getting on the bus my phone was still acting up. My first bus driver was an older lady from New Orleans. I think she could tell that I was a fish out of water and she gave me the best advice she could in regards to me getting to my destination. She told me I was only in need of catching one more bus and I could ride that one out towards the end of its route and then I would be in West Hollywood. I was a little sad that her route did not go that way because she gave me a temporary sense of comfort; almost like a long lost aunt. Getting off her stop, I was around the UCLA campus but my phone was dead, and it took way longer to get there than expected. So as expected, Ish was already gone.

I walked to the bus stop and just waited for my bus to come up and it seemed like forever. In the meantime, I realized that I was not in North Carolina to say the least. California was a lot faster and more diverse. I just remember thinking that I had not been around this many different people at one time in my life. It was a short lived joy as my bus finally came and I asked the driver about my stop and the driver said it was the second to last stop and would take roughly another hour. Clearly, I was irritated at this point, and I just remember sitting down in my seat and looking out the window with tears in my eyes thinking, "Lord how in the world did I end up in this situation–being across country with no money and traveling under such abnormal conditions?" The one thing that kept playing in my head was to trust God and my dad saying, "Even when you aren't happy you can always be grateful." I then saw a sign for Beverly Hills and I cracked a smile. The day before, I never would have thought I would be in California, near Beverly Hills?

After I finally got off at my stop, I walked down about five blocks to Ish's apartment. I heard his voice from the parking lot looking out the window waiting for me. Ish was my boy. Not only did we grow up together playing basketball, but our friendship also grew during our college experiences. Ish was a Capricorn just like me. Him, Bobby, and Fatboy Josh; all of our birthdays fall behind each other and it makes me think that people's personality type is somewhat tied to their zodiac sign because of the traits we all share as Capricorns.

One of the things about us Capricorns is that once we are in our element we can go into full blown character mode, and it usually takes one of our friends to do it. So of course as soon as I got up with Ish, it was nonstop laughs. I told him that I was hungry and I need to get something to eat, and I wanted something that I could not find in NC. He told me not to worry and that after we finished eating, he was going to take me around to show me the city. Serendipitously, Winston "came through" with the money, so now I could make the best of my time in California before my return to North Carolina. Our first stop was Hollywood Hills.

Canyon Run is a popular area where a lot of people bike and trail run too. It offers one of the most amazing views over Los Angeles. I asked Ish to stop the car, and I got out and walked over to the edge which was blocked with a fence. I stood there and felt my eyes get watery. I felt God tell me, "if I can bring you across the country for you to enjoy this view of perspective, then when will you let go and just trust me?"

That moment was certainly a defining moment in my

faith. Leaving the area we went down to Hollywood Blvd which gave me a funny feeling in my stomach. It was the type of feeling that makes you uncomfortable but there really isn't a particular thing you can point out that makes you feel that way outside of the atmosphere in general. I think it was all the celebrity lookalikes that creeped me out. Some of the lookalikes look just like who they were pretending to be.

The next day my college friend Jasmine drove up from San Diego to take me back to the airport. Jasmine was a cheerleader at NCCU and she dated my line brother Josh. At the same time I was dating the captain of her cheerleading team, so we use to confide in each other about each other's situations while we were in school. Neither one of us stayed in our relationships, but we managed to maintain a pretty strong friendship that evolved after she enrolled into the military. Using my military background and expertise, I gave her the best advice I could during the process and ultimately, she chose to go. On a side note that is the reason her and Josh broke up. It had been a few years since we last saw each other so we spent some time catching up and then we spent some time reminiscing.

All the time I spent gum yapping turned into me forgetting about the application. I had not filled out Winston's application and I still had to complete Brandon's application so our reunion turned into us sitting outside in her bright orange camaro filling out the applications so I could put them in the mail while I was still in Los Angeles. I will always appreciate her help because it was a lot, and throughout the duration of us working, she continuously stated that she did not sign up for this.

Good thing she got that good education from NCCU. We finally got finished and was about to put the applications in the mail and head to the airport. Jasmine had planned to take me to lunch, but the application took so long that she had to just drop me off at the airport. When people ask me, "why won't you move to a big city," I bring up this story because Jasmine and I were stuck in Los Angeles traffic for over an hour and we were just blocks away from the airport. I missed the required thirty minute pre-check in protocol and was told I could not catch my flight out. I was moved to another flight that instead of putting me back in North Carolina that night would have me flying over night and landing early in the morning.

Jasmine   Runyon Cayon

I had to call Jasmine to come back and get me and we had about a 4 to 5 hour window before my next flight so we drove around the entire city and went sightseeing. At that time I smoked Black and Milds, so I guess you can say we had a smoke out on Black and Milds while driving through the city. She dropped me off back at the airport, and just like that my trip to LA was ending. Before I left I sat outside of LAX listening to J Cole daydreaming about the day I would return to Los Angeles and how I would return to North Carolina as a "King."   That season of Shark Tank they had used segments of what we had shot that night in Greenville as promo commercials, and there were about six of them. So the entire season of Shark Tank I would get random text messages or in-boxes about someone seeing me on Shark Tank and when would my episode air. By this point, I pretty much knew that because we did not have what the application they were looking for that things would never be. It was a bittersweet feeling. It's almost like making it to the finals but not winning the championship.

Chapter 15: *Sideline Story*

I made it to the rack, even though they tried to box me out
I got the key to the game, they tried to lock me out
But what they don't understand is this is all plan
It's a bigger picture and you can't photoshop me out

-J.Cole (Sideline Story)

9th Wonder

Returning to North Carolina, getting ready for my last semester of graduate school was something I was looking forward to. The enjoyable thing about graduate school was right as I was getting sick of it, it was about to end. I continued to enjoy the seclusion the library offered me and I spent a lot of time there. At this time my cousins had moved out so there was about a three week window where I was sleeping at my girlfriend's house, Brandon's place, and my house which had no running water and no electricity. Towards the tail end of this window, I started sleeping in my car because of the smell in the toilet in the house, times were rough. I was never raised like this.

But luckily for me, I survived and when school started, I got my refund check!! That's the second thing I enjoyed about graduate school, the refund checks! Brandon and I found a sublease apartment we were able to rent for six months. It was a basic two story townhome on the back side of an apartment complex but for two brothers who just survived not having a living situation at all; this was just as good as the Ritz Carlton.

Moving in we never put furniture down stairs in the living room, and we did not have a TV in the apartment. We called it the "trap," which became an issue once Duke Basketball started. I would go down to a bar down the street to catch the game. I loved the fact that we didn't have a T.V though because we had fewer distractions. I had my wall covered in my accomplishments and few ideas to try to motivate me everyday to become the person who people perceived me to be. And I had started a routine of picking up my daughter every morning and dropping her off at school.

I had a rough semester that semester and prior to it, the assistant Dean Dr. Alston, who was the mentee of my God Father which used to ironically was the Dean of Agriculture, gave me a good tongue lashing about not performing well because the bar of excellence was higher for me. I was just grateful that they didn't kick me out and gave me the opportunity to finish what I had started.

By this time we had also formed a relationship with Mr. Valee Taylor and Taylor Fish farm. Mr. Valee's tilapia farm is only one of two in the country and only one of four in the entire world. It was also the only operation on a commercial scale that I could get experience working in. I had met Mr. Valee a few years back through the internship that I had at NCIMED and through one of my boy/business partners at the time Antonio F. We tried to do some work for Mr. Valee, but nothing ever came of that moment.

I caught up with Mr. Valee a few years later at an Executive Networking Conference (Durham, NC) and he told me that he had just gotten his tilapia into Whole Foods and that he was working on a few more deals. I don't know if he thought I was bluffing or not, but at the time I was in graduate school and I was looking for an opportunity to work for free if I had too. I gave him my information, and he said he would contact me. While we were there, he gave me some mentoring advice about networking and I took him up on it, and I actually got to shake hands with Representative G. K. Butterfield. As I was taking the picture, Mr. Valee walked up with a big grin on his face and gave me the "thumbs up" sign.

I should mention that those networking tips helped me to introduce myself to Bob Brown, the Chairman of B & C Associates. He is a legendary man who served in the Nixon Administration and is one of the driving forces behind MWBE policy giving countless minorities the opportunity to do business with any projects funded with public dollars. His company also has done countless missions in Africa to provide education and books along with services. To fully understand all of Bob's accomplishments, you have to look him up on your own.

Anywho, I walked up to him and he was standing with Thomas Snith, who is the Chief of Staff to the governor. I introduced myself and told him who my dad was. He cracked a smiled and looked at Mr. Snith and said, "I used to do business with his dad." I asked for a picture and was granted one and I asked him for a business card and he told me he would be in touch. Walking away from that night Mr. Valee had given me a lot of confidence that I took to heart, but he never called me. Ironically, later that year Mr. Perkins called me into his office and said: "Matt there is a fish farm for sale in Orange County and I think we should look into purchasing it for the food hub." As he continued to talk, I realized he was talking about Mr. Valee, so I paused him and said his name and he said, "well yes, his fish farm." That led to my immediate confusion. Mr. Perkins looked at me and said, "Well I think he is selling it because he has developed cancer."

I was blown away. Mr. Valee looked like he was in perfect health just months before. Mr. Perkins said he had an investor friend he wanted to introduce me to, and he wanted all of us to take a trip down to the fish farm. The friend ended up being David Couch, a real estate tycoon who also had a small agriculture empire as Mr. Perkins liked to call it. For whatever reason Mr. Couch and I hit it off; we really connected on a lot of random topics. He was a former football player at Wake Forest so we had a lot of guys talk to break the ice.

We drove down to the fish farm, and he met Mr. Valee, he was super impressed with the operation. He just kept saying, "We have to get your story out. We have to get your story out!" He mentions a friend he had that he wanted to bring to the fish farm named Armstrong Williams. Now initially I had never heard of him but the way everyone else made it seem, he was a big-to-do. Mr. Couch said he wanted to set up an interview with Brandon and I and that he would be in contact with us when it was time.

About a month passed before we got a phone call from Armstrong Williams's office telling us we were scheduled to be interviewed and to get ready. The morning of the interview Mr. Perkins called me and said something came up and that he would not be able to come to the fish farm until later and to meet David at the airport to pick up Armstrong Williams. So Brandon and I headed to the airport to meet David, and when we arrived we also meet another gentleman named Bill Millis. I was thinking that I was meeting new people, so I just shook his hand and introduce myself and David said, "Let's all ride in my truck together." A few minutes later, Armstrong Williams walked out the airport with one of his assistants. We all greeted each other and hopped in the truck.

It wasn't until I got into the truck that I realized who I was riding with. I knew that David had money, and I also knew that Armstrong Williams was a television and radio political personality. I had no idea of his wealth. He was telling us about hotels he owned overseas and closing million dollar deals, and once he was done David said, "Now Bill tell them who you are." Bill looked at me modestly and said, "Oh my family runs a small sock factory." David chuckled and said, "that small sock factory is worth millions." Bill just smiled, but once we begin to talk, all of them seem pretty interested... none more than Bill.

No one cut an investment check that day. Once we got to the fish farm we were told to go inside to get our makeup done. The crew set up the cameras for the taping outside. Although I wasn't really nervous, this would be one of the biggest personality interviewing me thus far, so I wanted to make sure I did a good job. Brandon and I were interviewed separately and our topics were on young entrepreneurs. Once we were finished, he interviewed Mr. Valee, his sister, and then David. Mr. Perkins had arrived towards the tail end and I had thanked him for introducing me to David and for this experience. Although, I don't believe Armstrong Williams actually aired our interview, that doesn't take away from the fact that it happens.

During this time we were also negotiating the start of our mobile Oasis Farmer's Market. Over the summer my nonprofit, Vision Tree, received our EBT certification and worked with the county health department to develop a mobile market trailer that was funded by the local United Way. They gave us seventeen thousand dollars to retrofit the trailer unit in order for it to be an operational mobile market. We were to run a nine week pilot project in which Brandon and I would be the mobile market managers. We would be working for free;

however, I was able to use the experience in my capstone project for graduate school so it all worked out well.

Our first day started on October first outside of the health department parking lot. It was very exciting to see something that we had spoken about for over a year finally manifest. We had a lot of media coverage and prior to that night, I had heard the radio personality on the gospel station reading out our press release. Things were definitely starting to get surreal for me. The next day we had a line of customers waiting for us to open. This was our morning stop, and it lasted from eight thirty to eleven. Most of the customers were employees from the health department which is an aspect I need to stress because the economic lines have been blurred so bad that people who work at the health department, who most would consider having a good job, were our most loyal customers and constantly praised us for our service and how beneficial it was to their schedule.

Our actual target market was the EBT population which is very diverse, but our population target was geared towards food deserts which were mainly located in low-income low privileged communities. Our second stop was in the Warnersville community at the city's recreation center in the middle of the community. This afternoon market would usually be less attended than the morning markets, but it was more purposeful in my opinion because these were the people who really needed our services. People enjoyed our fresh produce, and we started to make a big splash around the town.

We had a coalition of partners to push the project along: The Guilford County Health Department, UNCG, East Market CDC, United Way, Blue Cross Blue Shield, Moses Cone, and Hayes Taylor YMCA. They get mad at me when I don't list all the partners, but out of all our partners, we created a steering committee who would help guide decisions based around the mobile market. For the sake of discretion, I will leave the names out of those who made up the committee, but I will say Brandon and I were a part of it and our mentor, Phil Barnhill of East Market CDC was also there and severed as the fiscal agent.

I was very excited about what was going on but simultaneously the city of Greensboro had paired me up with this supposed to be investor who had taken me around the block for a year in getting funding for my urban farm City Oasis Project in Warnersville. I will certainly admit that I learned a lot from that situation, both good and bad, but what people did not understand from an inner circle level was that their complaints were unwarranted; they began to complain without the full context of the situation. One particular steering committee member acted very indifferently. This was probably because she had been working on the food desert issue prior to me coming back to Greensboro. Many of our ideas were the same, and I was younger with a social network that surpassed years of experience gained; I believe she found that challenging.

Another example was when another committee member revealed to me an opportunity to do a Ted X talk. At the time I was unfamiliar with the speaking platform but became very familiar with what it was doing and after I conducted my own research, I became a huge fan. I realized what this platform could do not only for the funding of my projects but to also put these issues on a national radar. I had planned to use my speaking ability to drive it home. I was practicing in the shower, talking to myself in the car, watching videos, and imagining how my presentation would turn out, the whole nine yards. But then something strange happened. The committee member who brought me the idea stopped talking about it. She didn't bring it up anymore, and I was confused on the timeline. So, I finally reached out to her, and she told me that they chose to go with the committee member that mentioned earlier. The bureaucracy was real.

So, I ate that misfortune and channeled my energy so that I could still be cheerful and cordial while keeping my displeasure about the situation to myself. A year later my lawyer revealed to me the same opportunity that was brought to me a year prior to do a Ted X talk came up again. I just knew that this time around it was going to happen, and I was going to get my shot. I had an entire year of progression and my presentation would now be infused with what I had been learning in graduate school. I could use this as a platform to explain my capstone project to a wider audience. My lawyer did inform me that it was a chance they could go another way because they had already covered the same topic year prior, but he ensured me that he would be pushing on my behalf.

And then something weird happened. We were in a steering committee meeting and I overheard the same raggedy member saying she was asked to come back and give an update Ted talk from her previous presentation. I was beyond myself. It took everything in me not to say something, but as soon as I got out of the meeting I called my lawyer and he confirmed that the council did decide to pick the topic back up but still wouldn't give me a chance to speak. That was the first sign of the writing on the wall. My time in Greensboro was coming to an end.

I worked very hard in my classes that semester and only had two difficult classes: pest management and another online class. I was able to survive the pest management class, but that online class was something else. The online class was with an old professor. The first time around with this professor, I thought that I was doing well in the class but then I had to hustle and bustle to get out of it. I swore that I would never take that professor again and then "BAM," I got him again. I will always cherish my relationship with my advisor Dr. English.

Much like Dr. Jones, she played a much needed motherly role for me during graduate school. With all the public expectations, Dr. English was really the only one who asked me, "Well Matthew, how are you taking all of this?" I can't even lie, when I sat down to talk to Dr. English about my apprehension about the online class and that old professor, my eyes filled up and I broke down. I had not cried in such a long time. My daughter's mother was giving me the worst time from our dealings, I was getting no help from the funding side of my projects, the expectations for me were through the roof. People were expecting me to turn water into wine and to provide diamond studded long stem glasses to pour it into.

Dr. English helped lessen my load by taking me off of the horticulture track and placing me strictly on the agriculture education track. This lessened my academic stress and gave me an opportunity to finish on time. Mind you, I've been doing the school thing since pre-kindergarten.

I promised myself that if I made it to my last semester in graduate school that I would take a trip to the Virgin Islands in January as a part of my capstone project. At the University of Virgin Islands, they have the largest experimental density farm lab on the east coast. They mainly focus on commercial scale operations that produce high volume, high quality, and high returns. The mobile market to me was an elementary step to solving the problems.

What was ultimately needed was a commercial scale density system to replace traditional farming. Traditional farming requires fresh water and land that we are running short of. At the same time, the population is rising and so is the cost of food. My idea was to go to the Virgin Islands to conduct research on how these systems could be implemented in empty warehouses and retrofitted into grow operations.

I was still dealing with the same investment guy, and it was going on for a year. We had been spinning our wheels on how to get funding and I had exhausted my network for the time being with no results. The only thing that came out of our year long business relationship was the relationship I gained with another investor he brought to the table. In his conversations with me, it was my understanding that they together would go in on investing in my company, and that they had about thirty thousand dollars in seed money for my company. The deal was contingent on me getting a life insurance policy as collateral. I understood that concept, and it was a business practice done at most levels of business when dealing with the executives. But at the same time, I didn't have anything to put up but my life, so I took it as fair is fair.

So in late September I went with the initial investor and took out a life insurance policy on myself and made him and the other investors the beneficiaries. From there I was under the impression that the thirty thousand dollars would be coming any day to give us some breathing room on our day-to-day expenses of bootstrapping this company. Months passed and there was no word of the investment money... not one word. We continuously had meetings and nothing resulted from them. By January I was kind of fed up. When I mentioned to him about me going to the Virgin Islands, he instructed me to go ask Mr. Robbie Perkins for the money. I thought to myself, "Why did I get an insurance policy then?"

Instead of blowing my lid, I took it all in stride and called the other investor later that night to bring my situation to his attention. I told him that I was trying to get to the Virgin Islands, why I was going, and the fact that I needed a little more than what I personally was brought to the table. He was confused. He said, "Matthew why are you coming out of pocket? I gave the other investor fifteen thousand in cash in September for these very purposes?" Red flames filled my eyes. I had gotten lied too, not only lied too but exploited for money, money that was only given because of my life insurance policy.

After I confronted him about the situation, he knew I caught him red handed. He didn't know how much I knew nor did I allow him to, but he knew enough that I knew he got money on my behalf and never mumbled a word about it.

These are the things that go on behind the curtains that nobody sees; the aggravating situations that are completely naïve to the fact that this is what I was dealing with business wise. I was really hurt, and I felt betrayed by the investor that I had grown to trust; or so I thought. In the end, he was just trying to exploit my intellectual property for his own gain. He was the first, but certainly wouldn't be the last

I ended up paying for the trip out of pocket through my school refund check. I take the second seat to no one in regards to the amount of effort I put into myself financially and in general to become such a successful person and a better man. I was blessed to be able to find something affordable and was looking forward to taking a break from the messiness of Greensboro.

Chapter 16: *So Ambitious*

So they made light of, my type of
Dreams seem dumb, they said wise up
How many guys-a, you see making it from here
The world don't like us, is that not clear? Alright but
I'm different, I can't base what I'm gon' be
Offa what everybody isn't, they don't listen
Just whisperin behind my back
No vision, lack of ambition, so whack!

-Jay-Z (So Ambitious)

The gentleman I was to meet was named Donald Bailey, and he was the cooperative extension agent on the island. I reached out to him weeks prior to my travels to inform him of my intentions, and he told me he would be more than welcome for me to come. The first mistake I made; however, was not staying on St Croix.

I was staying on St. Thomas not understanding the difficulty it took to get to those two islands. I was scheduled to spend three days with him, but ultimately, I only could afford one boat plane right to the campus. Once I arrived on campus, it was like the mountains crumbled, the seas roared, and the glow of heaven had descended upon this campus. My first stop was to the bookstore where I met the nicest lady. I can't remember her name, but she was so kind and helpful. She gave me instructions on how to get to my designation and even called a janitorial staff member to walk me over.

Once I arrived, I met Mr. Bailey in one of the greenhouses on site and I think one of the initial things that stood out was the fact that I called him a doctor and he corrected me disclosing he had only obtained his masters. That was very encouraging to me considering that I was starting my final semester of graduate school. That morning he gave me a tour of the site and explained how everything worked.

St. Croix Research Station   Donald Bailey

That took us up to lunch time where I was given a ticket to go eat in the lunchroom for free. On the way there I met some AKA's who were fundraising in the café, and I sat and ate lunch with them. They even gave me two more tickets to get more food. After lunch, Mr. Bailey and I worked out of a tilapia tank separating males from females. I honestly didn't ask for much, but to shadow him was such a great thing. He was constantly telling me, "I hope you are getting something out of this," and I thought to myself, 'yes, more than you can imagine.' Just being out there working was something else. It was quiet, it was tropical, and it was peaceful. I have not met all the people on the entire island to say that all of them are friendly, but the ones that I did come in contact with were some of the most sincere people I have ever met. Everyone that I worked with all saw this work as something greater than themselves... it was truly paradise.

I guess I had made such an impression on Mr. Bailey that he had even offered to take me back to the airport himself. We spoke about his career and his stay in St. Croix. He explained to me that because of the location of the research station it makes for an exclusive learning destination for companies and researchers from around the world. He was telling me about the time he was training with the Disney F Cot crew. And I was just thinking, "Wow that is such a dream job to have." Pulling up to the airport he gave me my good wishes, he told me to be in touch, and that he would be looking forward to hearing from me post-graduation. As I left St. Croix, I felt as if I would be back. It was a promise I made to myself.

I really enjoyed my stay in the Virgin Islands from the food to the culture, I was much more comfortable around those people for some reason. Maybe because I didn't feel the pressure of American Police, or maybe because the people's values weren't necessarily placed in capitalistic value, or maybe because those same people who gave me those life lessons were the same ones relaxing in their million dollar yachts.... To be wealthy and anonymous... that 'tis' the question.

The next day I headed back to the states vowing to return to the place that had given me the most peace I had experienced since my dad passed. One fun part of this story was the fact that I got on the plane with my island outfit on, shorts and short sleeves. I was just leaving eighty-degree weather, but it was so cold on that plane. I was miserable. If that was not enough, Duke had lost to Notre Dame earlier that week and the next day they dismissed my favorite player on the team. Around the time of my arrival in NC, Duke was playing Virginia at Virginia and they were undefeated at the time. I remember being at the luggage claim watching the last two minutes of the game. We had to come back from behind, and as we took the lead. Tyus Jones hit a huge shot to win the game, and I scream real loud and said: "Let's Go Home." I know people were looking at me like, "this crazy Duke fan wearing summer gear in thirty degree weather... he is loco."

Coming back home our lease had ended at the apartment and we were looking for a place to move into. At the time my girlfriend and I were getting serious about our relationship and we were planning on moving in together. We found a place in High Point and Brandon came with us for what was supposed to be temporary until he found a place of his own. That's the short version. The funny part of this was that this was the most obstacle filled move of my life. Starting with the move out; the apartment complex said that I did not pay for one month of rent, and I knew I paid for all my months of rent. I used my student refund check to pay my bill. Then it was the actual move; that was a circus of its own. World Star Hip Hop should have been there to catch all the follies, but you know what at the end of the day, I was grateful that the highest had blessed me with a newly remodeled home. I could finally have a room for my daughter. I was okay with a brother who was struggling to make a living situation workout period.

Business wise things were starting to come together in regards to becoming operational. We began to sell eggs from Caldwell County to a restaurant in Greensboro, and we were working with our tilapia farm. But the trip to the Virgin Islands had hurt my pockets, and I was in need of a financial boost. What I had was an opportunity to compete in a social entrepreneurship at NC A&T and representing the school's grad school team. We had been working with Dr. McEwing who was the husband of the dean of the school of business. He was very excited about our pitch and felt we had a chance to win.

To be fair, I had no idea how big this competition was. By this time I had won a few other pitch competitions around the city and was using them as a method to keep a few dollars in my pocket. Shark Tank had given me a lot of confidence and grad school was giving me a lot of ammo to backup my business concept with facts. Getting ready for the competition was much more was on the line this time. The winner took home five thousand dollars. The week before we had did two dry run pitches in front of A&T faculty for advice on how to improve our pitch. The night before Brandon and I stayed up late perfecting our pitch and going to sleep that night I knew we were prepared. And that was the most I could ask for.

The next day Shannon who was our other pitch partner told me she could not get off work, and would not be able to make the pitch. I told the staff of the competition and Dr. McEwing the situation. Both the competition heads, as well as Dr. McEwing, understood that Brandon was just my business partner and not a student like Shannon and I, and that it was within the guidelines of the competition to still compete, remember I said that. Arriving at the competition that day we were very focused and a tad bit overwhelmed once we saw how big the competition actually was. All sixteen schools were in attendance. The entire college system was represented and most of them were MBA students since this was an entrepreneurship competition.

Teams had matching outfits and deep numbers in their teams. It was just Brandon and I, but we were ready. That morning we had breakfast, and they had a guest speaker who spoke but I really couldn't take in a word he was saying because my anxiousness. The way the competition was broken down was we would all leave the big ballroom to go to classrooms where there would be four judges there to hear our pitch.

We had a little time to wait before we started but we could see all the school's advisors began to take bets on who the team would win, not literally bet, but just a little jabbing at their thoughts on who would win. We also felt a little pressure from the NC A&T staff and faculty there because the competition was hosted on NC A&T's campus and let me take the time to again remind everyone I am an Eagle at heart, so it was hard for me to swallow competing against my alumni.

I did my research prior to the competition on the judges that would be in attendance and there were two in particular that I wanted to speak to Marty Kotis and Dan Gerlach. Mr.

Kotis was a well off real estate broker who also owned restaurant concepts. And Mr. Gerlach as the president of Golden Leaf Foundation, which is one of, if not, the biggest agriculture base foundation in the state. I luckily had Mr. Kotis as one of my judges at the previous competition I had won but he had left prior to me getting a chance to speak with him. This time I would have his full attention and a pitch that we knew was strong.

Prior to walking into the room I felt like a ball player getting ready for a game, listening to J Cole and imagine myself killing the pitch, and as we walked in I could fill the butterflies jump up and down in my stomach. I spoke to Mr. Kotis reminding him I was the one who won the previous competition thinking it would give me brownie points with him, and it didn't. At least that's what I thought. After Brandon and I did a great job pitching our presentation he grilled us... hard. But we were able to answer all of his questions with confidence and clarity almost as if we had been practicing for Mark Cuban or Mr. Happy on one of their bad days. Afterward, Dr. McEwing who had sat in on the pitch, had come out behind us very excited and confident we made it to the next round. The next round was the top four out of sixteen who pitch in the big ballroom in front of everyone.

After lunch, we sat in the ballroom nervously waiting for the other rooms to finish their pitches and for the judges to render their top finalist. During the wait I saw Mr. Kotis, and I approached him seeing if I could get an insight on whether we made it to the next round, and his response in which I can't remember exactly how he said it, but I took it as if he was saying we did not make it but don't let the outcome discourage. He also stated that he would love to sit down and meet with us post this competition, and although that was something I had wanted I was crushed at the fact that in my mind he just told me that we lost. Walking back to the table I told Brandon what had happened and Dr. McEwing kept giving us the thumbs up in confidence that we did make it.

Finally, after what seemed like forever they announced

the finalist and on a projection screen they put up the four teams that had made it, and I be dang on if Triad Food Hub wasn't one of the four listed teams. Relief overcame me as I looked at Brandon. In my mind I thought, 'they messed up now because from the number of our listing we were going to be the last team to go.' And after hearing the other teams pitch, I knew it was our competition to lose but if we did what we had been doing, we had it in the bag.

Ironically, our pitch in the final round had been smoother than the previous rounds, I think Mr. Kotis warmed us up, but the questions that were asked in the question-and-answer portion were nowhere as difficult as what Mr. Kotis asked, and we were the only team that could speak with confidence about our financial projections and social environment impact. Standing on that stage I felt in my zone, the mic in my head felt right, seeing the facial expressions of the judges while we spoke was satisfaction for all the work we had put into our pitch weeks coming in, and it was gratifying to have the feeling of having the entire room hang on to my every word. While other teams pitched, you could hear sidebar conversations go on while they were on stage but while we were up there, you could hear a pin drop, and I loved every moment of it.

Afterward, it took some time for the judges to return with the results but luckily not as long as they took before as they input the winners on to the computer we felt very confident about the outcome. Everyone was congratulating us on our presentation although that did not translate into a win just yet. It only meant that people were impressed. The judge finally returned to the stage with the results and after announcing the undergrad winners they began to announce the grad school winners. The first runner up and runner up were announced and to my pleasure, the team I was concerned about was announced as the first runner up. The only other team left I knew did not do as well as we did but I was trying to contain my composure until I knew for sure.

Moments later the announcer said, "and this year's

2015 Social Entrepreneurship Competition is." Then the screen flashed and in big bold words.... TRIAD FOOD HUB popped across the stage, it was a very surreal moment. All I could do was throw my hands together and look up and say Thank You. One of the judges had pointed that out after the competition he felt he made a good choice with his decision solely based on how grateful we responded after hearing our name. That meant a lot to me because I wanted people to see that all of this was fueled by a higher power. Leaving the competition that day after all the pictures and congratulations, Brandon and I felt as accomplished as we ever had. Shark Tank was one thing, but that was us walking into something we didn't know what to expect from. We prepared and put a lot of time into this social entrepreneurship competition so victory made the journey that much sweeter.

We named our trophy Pam Grier because she was a bad shut-yo-mouth, but our bliss was short lived. The next day the board of trustees at NC A&T wanted to present us at their monthly meeting and we were asked to submit our resumes and again, at the start of this I said Shannon and I were students and it was known by competition officials that Brandon was neither a grad student nor an A&T student at the time. So when NC A&T saw that he was an NCCU graduate they called Dr. McEwing to inform him that NC A&T did not want to accept the award, and they wanted to forfeit the victory for the sake of the "integrity" of the competition.

When Dr. McEwing called me to tell me the news, I thought it was a bad joke being played on me. I was crushed and angry. I could not understand that if the competition officials did not have a problem with us winning, why would NC A&T do this. I was given no further explanation only instructions to return Pam Grier back to campus as soon as possible and more importantly to us no five thousand dollars.

Looking back at the moment I can't even say how I recovered from not getting the money, but it's funny because that's how God works most time.

Most time we can't even remember all the times he brought us out of a situation we didn't know how we were going to get out of, only for time to pass and you not even being able to remember the details of our stressors. Guess that's God's way of helping us remember not to sweat the small things. In the greater scheme of things, he took away one award only to follow up with a bigger one.

The next month Ms. Harris was having her annual Executive Networking Conference in Raleigh, NC and I had been interning for her for the past three years and always volunteered my services for the conference, so I didn't think anything out of the ordinary when her assistant Ms. Maggie called me and told me that she wanted me to be at the conference. So I went through my regular routine for preparing for the conference, but then something strange happen. My sister called me and she was explaining to me how my mother would be in town the same time the conference was, and that they wanted to see me since she had transferred to Shaw University down the street from the conference. What I took for just abnormal talk was really the secret that everyone involved with the conference knew about... everyone but me.

This year's conference was shortened from three days to two days, and each conference is highlighted by the Executive Networking Dinner named after Willie Deese who is a top executive for Merck and one of Ms. Harris's Board of Director members. I had worked the conference for the past few years so most of the attendees were familiar with me and what I was trying to accomplish. This was the first year I had business cards of my own. That night preparing for the dinner my sister called me to tell me that she was coming to the dinner... again, this was strange because we had no prior discussion about any of this, but I just rolled with it.

The dinner had started and right before everyone started eating the President of NCCU's Alumni Association pulled me to the side and told me my old fraternity advisor, Brother Gregory was on his way and needed my assistance. By this time Brother Gregory had retired from NCCU and his health was on the decline. He was now permanently walking around with a breathing machine and needed to be in a wheelchair if he was traveling long distances. But this is the guy who took the chance on me back when I first got to NCCU so I would do anything for him including run in the rain to get him, which I did.

It almost seemed as if only an hour had passed and the sky had opened up and it was pouring down something hellish. Walking out in my formal attire I had no umbrella and Brother Gregory managed to park his car far enough that I was able to get soaked. But we were happy to see each other, and we exchanged laughs and updates all the way to the door. Then something strange happened, Mrs. Gunn came looking for me.

Now Mrs. Gunn was Ms. Harris's second in command with Mr. Ali, and she was kind of the no nonsense person of the office but I always adored Mrs. Gunn and wanted to be as impressive to her as I did Ms. Harris in a lot of ways. But when Mrs. Gunn is looking for you... you know you are being looked for.

She came and told me they needed me back in the ballroom, and I just figured they needed help sitting someone down or moving a table or something but walking back into the ballroom I look at the two projection screens in the room, and above it said, "NCIMED 2015 Young Entrepreneur of the Year." I was beside myself as you can imagine. I was standing there soaking wet with the entire room looking at me and my sister sat there with the biggest Cheshire Cat grin on her face. She had got me. She knew the entire time. I did notice;

however, my mother wasn't there.

I walked to the stage where Ms. Harris and Mr. Ali were standing and Ms. Harris began her monolog of our journey, how I came to her three years prior, and how I had developed to that point. I wish I could remember word for word what she had said, but I was in utter shock. The gravity of the moment was overwhelming. As she wrapped up, she commissioned me to the mic and, as she had done so many times before she instructed me to deliver my elevator speech.

I did, although in my shock, I can't even recall what I said. But people gave me a standing ovation, and at the moment, the intern who each year watched panel after panel get up and speak and dreamed of his day of being on stage finally got his chance. The first thought that popped into my head was, "boy–if my dad could see me now?" Brother Gregory made his transition a few months later. I am so glad that he got to see me in one of my finest moment.

After the dinner I continuously thanked him, telling him that I would not have made it without him. I helped take him back to his car and then I headed straight to my hotel room. When I got to my hotel room, I just sat on the bed holding my award and cried like a baby. I didn't know what I did to deserve it. I had felt like I hadn't accomplished much but through it all, I missed my dad and my mom.

The next morning I ran into Ms. Harris. I hugged her tight and assured her that there was no way I could ever repay her for what she had done for me. She had a somber look on her face and asked if I had talked to my sister about my mom attending last night, and I told her my sister had mentioned that my mom was there but didn't say anything beyond that. Ms. Harris told me that when my mom found out about my award, she had Beth called Ms. Harris to see if she could get a free ticket as well. Ms. Harris not being the biggest fan of my mother for obvious reasons told her she could purchase a fifty dollar ticket to attend.

Now from my perspective, Ms. Harris was within all of

her rights to tell her that for the fact that Ms. Harris had been my mother for the past three years. Everything that I was supposed to be going to my mother about, I was going to Ms. Harris about. Her being the psychology major, she is saying that I had problems asking for help, and that I would rather go without than ask for help. I think my mom had made me self-conscious about asking for help because I knew I couldn't get any from her. I guess I always felt as if I wasn't deserving of any help for whatever reason.

I Guess it was sort of some post-traumatic stress from our relationship? But Ms. Harris always over-extended herself to assure me I was never alone. To this day she introduces me as her "son." I can't lie and say I wasn't hurt my mother chose not to pay the fifty dollars to see me accept my award. It left a bitter taste in my mouth, which plays a lot into the tagline of my title. I never thought my mom getting married again would mean I would lose my mother as well It's funny that many people view me as popular, but very few noticed that I usually have the smallest cheering section out of all of my peers. I begin to realize my challenge in life was to manage the thought of the one person you want to have in your corner possibly never being there.

I often get frustrated with the absence my parents with thoughts like, "If this was how it was going to be why decide to have a child in the first place?" With my father I always felt like he left me. I know people go through storms and scandals, trials and tribulations, but I asked him specifically not to leave me after I found out he had tried to commit suicide the first time and he did, anyway? With my mom, I wish she had treated me the way she treats me with this amount of neglect now my entire life so that at least I could always say well that's just her. But to have my former best friend, the one who never missed a basketball game, the one who told me when I was a child that I was special and handsome when I felt fat and unwanted, the only person growing up that could look at me and tell exactly how I was feeling; to not have her anymore was a pain that was hard to mask. It was easy for people to say, "oh you just gotta learn to live with it." But the bittersweet reminder of all of my accomplishing moments was to not have my parents there supporting me. The support I know I would have received from both of them had my dad never died.

After coming back to Greensboro, I was rejuvenated to finish the semester and finish the urban farm project in Warnersville. By this time we had been notified that we had received a hundred thousand dollar grant, and it was an exciting time around the project. Prior to the grant everyone was all saying how they couldn't wait to pay Brandon and me for all the work we had done since we were literally the only ones who were part of the steering committee but worked the entire market for free. But something strange happened, I notice that we were getting closer and closer to the market season and I had not seen a budget nor had anyone discussed to us about getting paid.

As I would come to find out, some members of the committee had already met and split the grant up without allocating any money for Brandon and me. Not only that, but they also were talking about interviewing for the market managers positions. I was in total disbelief. I sent a message to one of the committee members who was in charge of the grant and expressed my concerns. Now, in my opinion, I didn't get nasty, but I did voice my displeasure in becoming an outsider all of a sudden once the money came. He responded in the most despicable email I have ever received from a cohort. He told me how I was over my head, and how I didn't know the kind of monster a federal grant size of this magnitude required.

Prior to the email, I had been optimistic that finally, I would have some funds to accomplish what I wanted to do at the urban farm, but suddenly I realized that it was not his intention for me to use a dime of this money for my motives at the project site. I spoke with Ms. Harris and she sent him an email response. She cc'd me on the email, but I never opened it. Let's just say we had no other issues between him and me directly. I guess his justification was the fact that things were not progressing as fast as they expected me to move... but you know what?

They had no idea about the fifteen thousand dollars, or the whole year I waited for that moment, or the fact that I really didn't have the big million dollar trust fund everyone expected me to be working out of, but I truly boot strapped every single part of our operation. But after one meeting at the project site for the urban farm in which I gave out positions and charted some objectives. I guess he felt as if I was overstepping my bounds, and in his email he made that clear.

So instead of blowing my lid, I simply called Phil and told him the situation. I told him that I will always appreciate the mentorship he gave Brandon and I and for always being up front with his intentions in the project because it's my belief that they wanted to bring Phil's nonprofit in more of the fold in order to marginalize the need for us even more. But he would not allow that to happen and reminded them of their commitment to pay us as market managers prior to the grant coming. After all, the grant was based on the EBT/SNAP program in which my organization was the listed handler of the EBT account. For our involvement in obtaining the grant, I couldn't understand why I was fighting to get paid?

After that, the team I was working with at the project site started complaining about how the committee member was treating them and speaking to them. I was given all the emails that were sent and was I highly upset at the tone and manner in which the member was talking to the team. Not only that, but I was given evidence of the member changing up the planting schedule and reverting planned plans without proper communication, almost as if this was their way of getting at me and my perceived abrasive approach. This forced me to conduct a take back at the urban farm site, which hurts because I really wanted to finish what I had started, but I couldn't. Not at that moment, not under those circumstances.

In the midst of the moment, it was hard for me to devote my undivided attention to the site because I was still finishing graduate school, and more importantly, my capstone project was my blueprint for the urban farm site.

I was again having a rough time in the same older professor's class and after a while, I found the basis of his displeasure with me. When I initially arrived, there was another guy in the city trying to pull a similar project off. I never felt quite comfortable with him so I never partnered with him. But the initial investor I spoke about, I should have taken it as a sign that their relationship went up in flames. In the midst of it, the investor was playing both sides of the fence and being that he was working with the professor it drew a line in the sand when it came to our projects.

I did excellent on my capstone project and scored very well on my exit exam. I remember collecting money for my graduation fees and cap and gown, which my mom bought for me and it meant a lot. The feeling of completing graduate school was surreal; something I couldn't put in perspective until the morning of graduation.

This time around graduation felt different. The rehearsal was different, the people were different, even the robe was different. Side bar, they asked me to model how to properly put on the cap and gown in front of the entire graduating class, so you know I was lit. It was sinking in by then, little by little, it was sinking in, "Imma about to graduate."

Mom and Beth   Cuzo PJ

The next day at graduation when I saw the excitement of the graduates, it was such as special moment for me. This would be my second graduation at the coliseum and this one was much larger than my high school graduation, but it felt full circle to be walking back across the stage in my hometown. I got a lot of random texts and social media shout outs from people who knew me, but did not know I was graduating from graduate school. I was really happy because my mom had come to the graduation.

Graduation was a very long ceremony, especially for me because NCCU does their grad and undergrad ceremony separate. NC A&T did them all on the same day, but luckily graduate students went first. Rep. John Lewis was our speaker, and I took to heart his message to use our degree to get into "good trouble" as he called it. He also challenged us to use our degree to progress our communities. As our names were called, I can remember looking up and saying, "God, you are amazing!" Once graduation was over, we were able to fully focus our attention on the mobile market which was scheduled to kick off just two weeks after graduation. We were looking forward to the season, and we sent out marketing ads on city buses around the city so it was cool for people to send me pictures of them seeing the signs and associating the project with me; which will become an important factor in the near future. By this time relationships had been established at the health department that rivals any other office and work relationships. Our project was no different.

After the budget mess, we had more fireworks the day of the market when we learn that our EBT machine was off line. I am not complaining when I say this, but to me it's funny how I was just always an afterthought until something went wrong. So as I was trying to gather information about our EBT status, we had political figures there as well as media and a lot of eager customers and to top everything off our grant had a program where we matched people dollar for dollar up to twenty dollars for each EBT purchase waiting. But the unfortunate circumstance was that our EBT machine was down. Reflecting back on the situation, I think they will develop an appreciation for what Brandon and I was able to make happen in the midst of the EBT situation. I will always be appreciative for Brandon having my back and handling business. We were able to survive the opening day hiccups.

During the next steering committee meeting, I suggested to the farmer who was supplying our markets EBT machine until we were able to get our back online we cannot move forward with our machine. It was agreed, and after speaking with the farmer everything was set. So for the next few weeks we began to utilize his machine until I was able to figure out what was going on with our machine.

In the midst of this we are getting crazy publicly for the project, but I notice less and less our names are being mentioned. Be it as it may a lot of work was put into this project from all the partners, but to be clear when it comes to functionality of the project there was only one market the entire season that neither Brandon nor I have to work, we made the project run and we knew it. We were blessed with wonderful interns and staff to work with but they could tell when our vibes were off. When the steering committee rubbed us off the wrong way; which was often, things were just off.

One consistent issue was the use of the term everybody eats, which was a conversation I was not initially part of. But it was between one of the committee members and Brandon. From the conversation that they had it was a collaboration to come up with the term and although Brandon is the one who came up with the exact saying from a longer saying they were initially trying to use it. Now anybody familiar with our culture knows exactly why and where Brandon got that term from and if you have never seen Paid in Full, I would not expect for you to get the meaning of why he said it either. From that conversation we chose to start our own social media pages to represent our portion of the project and we were going to run with everybody eats because of the cultural acceptance of the term with our peers.

The beef begin to become apparent when Brandon and I notice the committee member throwing shade on our social media efforts, stating that we pretty much didn't have the expertise to do what we were doing and that we should stream line our media pages. But we were thinking, 'well you are the communications expert.' There is no reason for our pages to be out performing yours. If they are local followers or not, we were building a self-made platform for ourselves and they did not like it. The member asked to take us out to lunch to hash some things out. I thought it would have been a good time to bring up the Tedx talk this person did, but I chose to just listen at first… just listen.

Mobile Market Crew

During the conversations I felt as if progress was made. I opened myself up a little about my personal situation as well as some of the circumstances that happen around me falling back from the project site. The member said they agreed that the other member had been acting irrational and that the project was at risk of losing community support. By this time all three of the team members had either quit or been fired. So, as we spoke I felt as if I was building trust. I was so wrong.

As the season continued, we began to expand our market. We started with two stops and were working on four additional sites. We were throwing a few floating sites in and around the permanent sites and at this point, the farmer's produce started to lose its quality, the fruit especially. We were getting complaints about the watermelons and the peaches. My complaint to the committee was the fact that those were our biggest sales during the summer. I was also very upset at the fact that the farmer kept dropping off boxes of rotten peaches. He did not even bother to open the box up and check. What's more insulting is the fact that somebody packed those boxes and knew the product looked like that.

By this point, I was ultra-upset because the steering committee was not the ones catching the heat, Brandon and I were. The entire purposes of me going to graduate school was to gain the expertise to say what was and was not of quality to sell. For a few weeks it was as if it fell on deaf ears. Finally, after taking pictures and keeping a few boxes as evidence we were finally allowed to supply the fruit for the market. This wasn't such a big deal for us, but we knew we could make a few dollars on the side by doing this; no more than thirty forty dollars max per invoice. Through our food hub, we already had the capacity to fulfill any order necessary. We were growing up as businessmen though, slowly but surely.

After we connecting with Mr. Valee, we ended up making a deal where we would be selling fish for him on the weekends at the flea market down the street from his fish farm. This flea market was a rather large one and on Sunday; it was flooded with Latinos. And from a graduate student standpoint, it opened a completely new view on local food systems. Here I was witnessing the same people Republicans were complaining about operating within their own world. These people mainly dealt with their own kind, and if you were not exposed to it, you would have never known. At this flea market, you could buy anything from live chickens to getting your tires changed, from buying cowboy boots, to buying Pescado Fresco from two brothers.

The funny part of this story is the best part of our marketing was the fact that we were two brothers with Locs selling fish in Spanish. Brandon, for the most part, is fluent in Spanish and he taught me just enough to make the sale and to negotiate. We found that they were a lot more accepting of us because we were respecting them enough to speak to them in their language. People who stop and stare or giggled would get a Spanish response from us which translated into English as, "You laughing because we speaking Spanish?" That would crack them up. Eventually, we ended up getting very good at selling the fish. We were moving up to three hundred pounds on weekends. We treated it like our block, like we were in Miami with Pablo. "We had that work," and because it was—eat what you kill– with Mr. Valee, as long as the product was good, we always sold out… always.

At the same time, I learned a lot about the Latino culture

and their food systems. I came to understand that their labor was not only taking over industries like construction, but agriculture as well. They were becoming the cheap labor farmers could hire and were paid underneath the table to harvest and maintain their farms. This also gave Latinos access to farm produce within the country's borders no longer requiring them to have long logistical routes from connections outside of the country. The other aspect of their culture is that in Mexico, you rarely saw homes with refrigeration, maybe an ice box. But they prepare all of their meals fresh so the need to go to the market was frequent, most times weekly. This need for fresh food allows for less of a need for pesticides because they are not expecting for their produce to have an unnatural shelf life span. Because of this, their produce was a lot more fresh and flavorful than what you would find in most grocery stores and the prices were cheaper too.

So with this understanding, we were able to find reliable sources for peaches and watermelons which were a hit once we starting supplying fruit to the market. Now, most people would have a problem with this, but this would only be for the culturally limited individuals who do not see the duality of how the same people who complain about them being here are the same ones paying them under the table to do their labor. Sometimes it is hard to live in a hypocritical society when rules only apply to some and logic is not required.

With this proof of information I went back to the committee and pulled up the USDA definition of local food and it said that local food was "any direction in a four hundred mile radius." So in essence that made North Carolina eligible to exchange produce from Canada to Florida. This information satisfied the committee, and we were granted permission to continue providing products to the market. Now these funds were not coming from the allotted funds from the farmer we were using for the market I mentioned earlier. But he was told so by another employee of the health department that I didn't necessarily see eye to eye with, but I didn't care to either, but he ended up pillow talking with the farmer talking about things he didn't know but lighting the farmers fire I guess.

By this time we were up to five sites and on our way to opening up our sixth one. The last stop we added was the most sentimental to me because we did it at the new Hayes Taylor YMCA they had built in the city. That meant a lot to me, but in the midst of my excitement the day before we were to open the market, I got a call from another committee member who said, "Hey, Matt, there was an email sent out and I think we are about to get audited?" My face turned white as if I had seen a ghost... "Audit?!" "Audit who?" "Me?!" She said they were going to audit the entire project but the email that was sent over was geared towards me and that's all she would say. About a week passed, and I was still waiting to see the email and the health department was trying to find out answers.

Chapter 17: F.A.M.E

Tryna make it through the storm, should be makin' history
No feelin' sorry for me, keep ya pity and ya sympathy
Good or bad, take it like a man, whatever meant for me
How I did it make 'em hate my spirit, they wish they could kill it
And they'll take it however they can get it
Wanna see me full misery, walkin' wit' my head down
"Let's decapitate him, then we'll see if he can wear his crown!"

-T.I (F.A.M.E)

Corey and our little bro Omari Collins

Now it's just my principal to not say certain people's name because I don't desire to give them any more of my energy but the story as told me was that a farmer was approached by a Guilford county extension agent, who I thought was a friend and who was familiar with the project as the extension officer, asked the farmer how was the Market going. Based off that conversation the agent told the farmer to put it in an email and send it to him.

After the email was sent, the agent took it to his boss who like him was familiar with the project and the committee members and could have easily called any of us, but instead she took it to the county manager who behind closed doors brought the county auditor in to instruct her to audit our books. By this time the director of the health department had hit the roof and, all hell broke out at the health department.

There was a witch hunt underway and to that point, no one had even seen the email. The health department called the farmer to ask what was going on and in a modest tone he said he just "sent a few operational suggestions to the county because they asked how things were going." This same farmer had gotten paid from our project that same week so he was no longer in a bad space I suppose and was suddenly saying, "I didn't know that this was going to be the result of all of this."

From there, the county finally saw the email and without showing me, called me and said that it wasn't good, it wasn't true, but it wasn't good either. A lot of serious accusations had been brought against me but they were assuring me they knew they weren't true. They couldn't understand why the auditor was going so hard when we already had a financial review scheduled at the end of the project.

On top of all of that, it took the county a year to process a contract from the year's prior mobile market that had zero financial transaction, just some fancy memorandum of understanding agreements and our staff didn't get paid for half of the season because of how long the country took to process and allocate funds that they didn't even give us. My biggest issue was that everything had been a long and drawn out process but all of a sudden, the county had all the time in the world to ask for every transaction I ever made. Not only that, no one from the county even bothered to come visit the market, nor did anyone come to any of our meetings. So they had no understanding of the inner working of our project, but they had an email and that email was enough.

I still remember that Thursday arriving at Hayes Taylor to set up for our market and there were two committee members and Mr. Phil waiting for me. To be fair, the committee member who brought it to my attention, I really admire her. She was of Eastern Indian decent and I felt that we were culturally connected on a lot of topics. The other committee member was the same one I was having Ted X and other communications issues. The Indian committee member, let's call her "Mrs. A," said, "Hey, let's go inside and talk?"

Walking into the room we all sat down and "Mrs. A" looked at me and said, "Well, I think you need to see the email now." and she handed me a piece of paper and this is what I read:

John ****

As you know I have some concern about operations pertaining to the Mobile Oasis. As the primary producer Smith Farms, Donna and I have questioned several things that we cannot understand about operations of Mobile Oasis. On 5-20-015 we delivered our first order to the Mobile Oasis later that week we learned that Vision Tree had failed to pay licensing fee for their ability to accept EBT. It was our understanding that the grant was to provide high quality fresh local produce to Guilford County food deserts. On 5-27-15 we were able to lend our personal machine and license Mobile Oasis which worked for five weeks until Matthew King entered wrong passcode into the machine several times until it locked down. Furthermore, he deleted the mobile market application after which he kept my machine for six days until I called Alex Lewis, and told him that I would report it missing. Alex drove to High Point and picked it up from Matthew King and delivered it broken at 8:45 pm 6 days late. It took 27 days to have the machine repaired which we were unable to accept EBT, Debit Credit cards, Wick and senior vouchers both at our farm store and the Greensboro Farmers Curb Market. Furthermore, Matthew King delivered our machine two hours after their market was over and drove by my retail shop and dropped the machine off at my sons home who lives on the back side of our farm which does not make sense. Also, the Mobile Oasis could not accept EBT during the 27-day period. After this, the market was good until Friday, August 21, got an email from Alex Lewis that our contact information had been passed on to Matthew King for logistics and have not heard from him.

FootNote: Matthew called at 8 pm on 5-26-15 to ask about use of EBT machine on 5-27-15 which had already been procured via Alex Lewis, and he proceeds to ask me for a customer list of my former seafood company which is very valuable on the night before the largest delivery to the Mobile Oasis market and the Greensboro farmers curb market. I do not understand! We received PO# for the produce the first was 39,000.00, then three more each for 1,000.00 again I, do not understand. After our machine was missing and broken, we offered paper vouchers that we had to key into the machine. What a nightmare! There were incomplete card numbers, incorrect approval numbers even to the point of different signature from printed name on the same voucher. Still have three vouchers that did not clear and have expired sent emails of problem we have 10 days to clear no response. On 8-26-15 received email for order 8-29-15 which was a small fraction of an average order after further questions found out that Matthew and Brandon were buying produce from wholesale markets which was in direct conflict of the statement that was drawn up by Guilford County Health Department stating that we are local farmers and will supply fresh local produce to the Mobile Oasis that I signed as part of the grant. I hope that these issues can be helped as we are dedicated to helping the food issues that are here at home

Respectfully Submitted,

George ****

    I had prepared myself for what the letter might have said, but even that did no justice to the blatant slander of this letter and for him not to think that it would stir the response that it did was stupid. "Mrs. A" almost seemed as mad as me. Apparently, the auditors were raising hell at the health department to the point that some employees disclosed to me that they were fearful of losing their job.

    Now, whether or not that was going to happen was beyond the point. The principality about the matter was that it was completely uncalled for. It was unwarranted and moreover, it was disruptive. As they wait for me to respond, I took a few deep breaths. Honestly, I was not as mad as I thought I would be. I knew everything in the letter had either already been taken care of or was just flat out disinformation. Were there hiccups... absolutely? But instead of being credited for improvising to keep things going everything was my fault especially the things that were completely out of my control.

    Heavy is the head of who wears the crown. "Mrs. A" began to explain the order of how things came to her and Mr. Phil was adding input in regards to his confusion, but I wasn't for the confusion. I had the farmer's number in my phone and volunteered to call him myself and ask him what this was about, but everyone quickly discouraged my idea; although I thought it was a good one. The other committee member who

I was already was having trouble with begin adding their input as well. For a second it seemed as if we were all lost.

No one picked up the phone to call us to even ask us what was going on or to express any concerns? The letter was taken to county officials who held weight in the industry. This was a complete slap in my face, but then something weird happens, "Mrs. A" had mentioned a meeting that the Director had with the county manager and something was mentioned about the urban farm in Warnersville.

Now prior to this revelation, I knew who was giving all the initial disinformation and his motivation in doing so, but this person had no understanding of activities at the urban farm. Immediately I knew I was dealing with two rats. I immediately caught the fact that the person I knew gave the nucleus of the email didn't have anything to do with the urban farm and I brought that point up.

Then the usual suspect that I was having all the issues with raised their hand and started apologizing to me saying, "I'm sorry." Now that I reflect on this whole ordeal, I might have said it may have been influenced to push them to act like this towards me so basically they were given the bullets to shoot at me from people I was working right alongside of, which is ironic considering all the success we were having with that mobile market in the public eye.

Once she apologized to me whatever anger I didn't have earlier rushed to the front of my brain and I felt fire in my eyes. I felt betrayed; it was as if I was thrown under the bus. After that, I got up, left the room, stormed out of the YMCA, walked to my car, cranked it up, and drove off. I busted out into tears. How did my good will all of a sudden make me the target of the highest officials of the county office? I wasn't scared or afraid. That wasn't why I had tears in my eyes. My tears represented the clear writings on the wall that my time in Greensboro was coming to a close.

After a few more apologies the member walked off, but I was still hot as fish grease. I made it through the market and after we were done, I wanted to speak to the county manager directly. I was really upset at the fact that I had intentionally stayed out of the public eye for the most part outside of my projects. I kept a very low profile around the city. I didn't bother anybody but even in my efforts, I still felt like I was still fighting my father's battle. I called commissioners Ray Trapp and Carolyn Coleman to tell them about the situation and they schedule a meeting for us three and Mr. Phil to be able to sit down with the county manager.

This meeting was going to be the first time I had ever laid eyes on the manager, but I had heard a few complaints about things he was doing or the things he wasn't doing, rather. Prior to this meeting he had never called me, attended a meeting, nor had he ever came to any of the mobile market sites during our two seasons. But the word was that the auditor was going to come to one of the mobile markets next week and to look out for her. The day of the meeting the county manager looked exactly how I pictured in my head. As we sat down, Mr. Phil had all of our financial records ready for any questioning and to start, I went line for line and discredited everything I was accused of with vouchers from both Ray and Phil. The portion of the conversation about the actual email lasted all of ten minutes. He voiced his displeasure for the farmer as well and told me I did not have to work with him anymore if I didn't want to.

Come to find out because our project had won the county a national award he came off a lot more friendly than I expected. But let's be clear the health department put in the work on the behalf of the county, it was not the county manager taking the issue of being number one in the nation in food hardship serious and looking for ways to fix it, until our project was on this grant.

But all of a sudden our conversation turns into how our partnership could be sustained and he asked for my ideas of what I thought should happen and also gave ideas of what he wanted to do, which I had to discredit because the model he was pitching was no more innovative than the programs that were already available. Our meeting went on for about another forty minutes, and I can't lie I left the meeting feeling good but simultaneously feeling like the entire meeting had an undertone to it and it did. The manager wanted to, in my opinion, take over financial control of the project.

After we left out, I went back to talk to members of the health department and the tone was completely different. Prior to that day they continued to say they were only reviewing our financial practices, now they wanted to see every transaction we ever made. An audit department that just a few weeks before did not have to time to finalize a contract to pay the project staff but now they have time to implement a full blown audit. I was prepped that the next day the auditor was going to come and observe the market. I was told to act normal but to look out for someone looking out of the norm. The next day when I saw her I immediately knew it was her. Ironically she looked just like my mom.

She was wearing a black business suit and was walking around more like an inspector than a customer. I walked up to her and introduced myself. I told her if she had any questions she could ask me, and I made sure she had an excellent customer experience as we did for all of our customers. She came to the afternoon market as well. She asked me a few general questions about the market, but nothing in regards to the audit. Although she did call Brandon and ask him some questions, my beef was the fact that regardless of what they said, I was the principal subject of the email and that was the fire starter that brought all of this about. I was sort of ticked off by that.

About two weeks later we had an official review meeting with the auditors. Going into the meeting I told Brandon to record the meeting, which I still have, and with a room full of people (our committee members, the health department's accountants, and the auditor's), you could cut the tension in the room with a knife. Once I sat down, I could feel my heartbeat pumping fast and my nerves began to shake a bit. I had to take a few deep breaths. Luckily, I did not intend to say too much; I really just wanted to hear them say that the email was the reason that this audit happened. As the auditors began to talk, I think they notice that they did not have many friends in the room and the funny thing was that beyond all of our work related issues, amongst us, this audit actually brought our committee closer together.

It was almost as if it was okay to fight with each other, but not okay to fight us all, and that is exactly what they did.

The auditors were talking about the protocol in which they reviewed our books and they were trying to sugarcoat the chaos they had created. Phil who was a much more seasoned businessman than I asked the auditors if they considered this an audit and they said they did not, only a review of our practices. He then asked what would constitute an audit because in his perspective our projected was just audited. His point was that if there were any additional steps needed to make this an official audit, there would be nothing more to review. We had turned over every single transaction we had ever done. Shamefully, they admitted that the conditions and environment might have resembled an audit but then they said, "if we would have found something then it would have turned into an audit."

Immediately I looked the auditor who had just spoken as if she had two heads and said, "Ma'am, well let me first say that I do not appreciate the manner in which they conducted themselves and that they had members of the committee fearing for their jobs and that all of this was uncalled for." I then asked them to cut to the chase and tell us if they found any financial violations and they said, "they did not," So I proceeded to explain my relationships with city officials, my experience at NCIMED and my experience interning for our Mayor. I understood municipal protocol very well, and I knew this was out of protocol.

I proceeded to ask them from their perspective, how did we reach this point? They then spilled the beans and gave me exactly what I was looking for. The auditor told us that the county manager had called her into the office for a meeting already in progress with him and members of the cooperative extension including the director. They explained to her that they had concerns about the email and wanted her to look into the project. I looked immediately at Brandon when she said that and Brandon just nodded at me to let me know that we got what she said recorded. The cat was out of the bag. They sent a witch hunt to the project to pin something on me to justify taking the project over.

From that conversation, she continued to say that they did not find financial problems, but they did think we would be in violation with USDA for using our sourcing for food. I ensured her that we were well within rights because we are using USDA funding, we under USDA regulations, and that we could operate in a four hundred mile radius from our location. She looked at me for a second and then looked around the room and said, "Is that true?"

I was done at that point. I was the only person in the room with a Master of Science degree in Agriculture. No one else even had an agriculture background beyond our efforts. They ensured her that I was correct, but by that time I was finished talking for the duration of the meeting. I was pissed. When they would ask me something, I would just shrug it off. I didn't have anything else to say. Not to mention, I was the youngest person in the room. I fought for my seat at that table and for her to just openly challenge my expertise was just another spit in my face.

The meeting continues for about another fifteen minutes and as I felt the meeting dying down a little, I told the room I had another meeting to attend and proceeded to try to leave. As I was leaving, the auditor stopped me and asked if she could speak to me in the hallway. I wasn't in the talking mood, but I wasn't going to be ugly. As I walked towards the elevator, I hear her tell me how she had my back the entire time and she just had to play the game, but she truly had my best interest. I also I knew I called Robbie and Carolyn Coleman who had already called her and asked her what she was doing to me. So at this point that egg was on their face; she was just trying to save face at that point. She said she told the county manager that he had no idea how much work went into the project and how much weight was on my shoulders. It was nothing romantic about it. It was very much hard work for very little pay.

I stopped her and asked her if she knew that I had worked three/fourths of the project without being paid? My staff had worked half of the market without receiving a paycheck either. Of course, she was not aware. I told her I was just amazed at the time management of the county didn't have time to pay us, but they have time to render an auditor. I told her that I was truly offended that she had openly challenged my expertise in front of everyone and as an African American woman, I would have thought she would notice that I was fighting a fight prior to her coming into the picture. In my eyes, this lady was the tool they had tried to use to destroy my character. I ran out of words for her, and as I did the elevator door opened, and I left.

As I rode down the elevator, I thought about out of our hundred thousand dollars, thirty of it automatically went to our EBT incentive program. I was only getting paid twelve hundred dollars a month, and that wasn't even enough to cover my bills. We never made any more than three hundred dollars at any site so even if there was any money missing, we are not talking about a lot of money. To me everything was clear. My project was welcomed in Greensboro, but I wasn't.

On top of that, I was given a phone call by Mrs. Johnson who asked me if I had watched the city council meeting the night before, and I told her I hadn't. She instructed me to watch it and reach back out to her. What I saw was the final USDA report given by Greensboro. The same report that had two of the reporting parties call me to downtown Greensboro and for an entire hour and a half I gave me MOST of my ideas on how to improve Greensboro's food situation, not because I wanted the glory, but because I really wanted to help.

After not hearing back from them following that meeting I proceed to see one of the people who interviewed me stand up and begin to give the report. Another city councilman who had taken it upon himself to say he was going to help end food deserts (although he never gave me a call) begin to narrate the report they were going back to send to Washington DC's office, and strangely enough, I heard all of my ideas but my name nor my project was mention once... NOT once.

Now under most circumstances, I would have just brushed it off. But my project had just received two hundred thousand dollars from the USDA office. So, to send back an official report about what is going on around food insecurity in the city and not breathe a word about my name or project was very disrespectful, but as God would have it prior to them finishing up their presentation another city council woman Sharon Hightower asked "Well, what about Matthew?" and instead of giving me my fifteen seconds of fame, they ended up spending the next ten minutes of the meeting talking about my project anyway, and following up with Mrs. Johnson afterwards saying she was very upset not to see my project or name mention in the initial final report.

And then something strange happens. Two months before my partners in Everybody Eats Company Brandon and Austin had submitted our application to Forbes Magazine Under 30 World Competition. The day after the audit, Forbes Magazine e-mailed us and told us that our application had not been selected for the Under 30 list, but we had been selected to be an Under 30 attendee in Philadelphia. At the time we did not know what this meant, but we knew that it was big!

Austin had class so he couldn't go on the trip. That left Brandon and I to head up 95 north to do lunch with Forbes and best yet, this had absolutely nothing to do with our nonprofit. As a matter of fact very few people in Greensboro even knew about my the transition from Triad Food Hub to The Everybody Eats Company and as I was reading the writing on the wall telling me to get out of the nonprofit realm and go for-profit. It was also telling me my time in Greensboro was coming to an end, coming to an end faster than I could ever image.

Chapter 18- Don't Worry

Don't stress over nothing we can't control on our own
Some people live on the street, some starve in their home
And all that we need is a chance or maybe some hope
Something to let us know that we are not alone
Though I know you be feeling like it'll never get better
But I promise you that it's not gonna last you forever
To hell with being depressed, be light as a feather
And sooner or later It'll all be coming together, yeah

-Timo, Rock City (Don't worry)

So we got ready for Forbes, got business cards, booked our hotel, and rented our car. We were on the road to changing our lives. On the way up, I received another phone call from the school of business in the Virgins Islands. The Dean of the business school said my name was passed on by Donald Bailey, and he heard I was interested in doing research. I told him I was, and he told me that they had a new executive MBA program he thought I would be perfect for if I was still looking to come to the island. I told him I was and began to tell him a little more about my background. Once he heard I already had my Master of Science degree, he stopped me and said, "Well you already have your masters, never mind our MBA program. We have a Ph.D. program in Creative Leadership that I think you would be perfect for!"

I was considering either going back to the islands to do research or go to Duke to get my JD/MBA, but I had not considered my Ph.D. just yet. He left me intrigued. I could finally get the business degree I was seeking. I had one degree in history and one degree in agriculture so now it was time for a business degree. I really wanted some more polishing in the business so I could get more familiar with terminologies. I asked him how the program would benefit me and he told me that it was a global base program where I could do my dissertation and my research at the same time. He also told me that it would take me to different cities around the world allowing me to learn how to assimilate my concept into the global markets around the world. Ultimately, he said that I would become one of the authorities of the density farm system industry.

I was excited about that opportunity but it was overshadowed by our arrival in Philly. Coming into the city Brandon and I just kept saying how much we felt this was going to be a life changing trip, little did we know we were right. The first event was a social mixer for all the attendees and it was there that we realized what we had accomplished. Literally, we met young entrepreneurs from the entire world.

Africa, Asia, South America, Europe; you name it, they were there. It was the epitome of a worldwide conference.

During the event, a member of the conference staff spoke and told us that Forbes had assembled fifteen hundred of the brightest business minds of the twenty-first century. They assured us that this would be the only time we would ever be all together under the same roof. So, they encouraged us to get to know each other. They had provided each attendee a very nice laminated name tag with everyone's business on them. It was an easy way to spark up a conversation with a simple observation of the name tag following with a simple, "Well, what does your company do?"

Brandon and I thoroughly enjoyed the buffet style food and the open bar which turned into being a common theme at the entire Forbes event that conference. It was the turn-up. The first night, they had a dope vocalist. I thought it was Erika Badu singing when I first walked in and she was really good. Socially, it was obvious that Brandon and I were from the other side of the tracks. We kept getting comments like, "You are so Urban." We just laughed it off, but it was noticeable. We stood out, and nobody ever thought that when we started talking that we would be talking about agriculture. We enjoyed the rest of the mixer and headed back to our hotel room. The next day we headed back to the first official day of the conference. It was more than we could ever dream of.

Beyond walking around the building for thirty minutes because the location was different from the night before, once we finally got in, we notice it was a lot more investor companies in attendance. Not only that, but we were able to talk to Forbes staff from New York, Chicago, and Hong Kong who all told us that if we would just infuse a little more technology in our idea that not only would we be on the Under 30 list, but on their Forbes list in general.

At the conference, we were only voice and it would it would be an easy icebreaker for anyone else I wanted to meet for the remainder of the night. I begin to scroll through the list of choices they had, and it was rather bare. I was not familiar with one song on the first two pages. I found my saving grace, Jay-Z's 99 problems. I was sold. I signed up for that song and anxiously waited for my turn to come up. The Black Album was my favorite album, so this was a cakewalk for me.

As I walked up on stage Brandon brought the IPad up to record. I went straight into party hosting mode getting the crowd involved, and then I proceeded to do my best Jay-Z performance of my life. The one I've done many times before in front of my mirror or watching Fade to Black. Once I said, "If you having girl problems I feel bad for you son, I got 99 problems but," and the crowd finished my sentence.

For the length of the song, I felt like I was Shawn Carter. Barring a few miss words in the last verse I really played the hell out of his second verse especially since we were one of the few tokens in the room. The rock band behind me gave it a good feel and at the end of it I was accused of being a professional. I think it was because I was one of the few who could stay on beat with the song.

And as I imaged, it was the easy ice breaker for me for the remainder of the conference. Honesty, everyone knew me as the guy who was rapping Jay-Z.

After having a blast that night we got ready for the last day of the conference with total confidence and many business cards in hand. It was exciting to head back to see what else we could get into, and it didn't take long. That day we happen to meet the Owner of Mitchell and Ness just parking our car. When we got into the conference, there was a buzz about ASAP ROCKY performing that night. We had a mobile market the next day, so we did the responsible thing and just did some networking prior to hopping on the road back to NC.

Later that week after getting back my big bro Chris Lea, "Sho Smoove," invited us on his radio show on 102 to talk about our experiences. It was a humbling experience to receive as much love as we did that morning because the host airs at six o'clock on Sunday morning so you don't expect that many people to be up. I think it finally sunk into Brandon and me what we had actually accomplished. I mean again we know Forbes and more importantly, Forbes now knows us.

While we were wrapping up the radio show, an older guy who graduated from NCCU showed us mad love and told us how proud of us he was. He kept saying how young were and that we were ahead of the game which in my mind sounded crazy because I always feel as though I am late.

Sho Smoove and Bunky   At the High Point Market

There were only a few weeks left in the mobile market and it was obvious everyone was counting down the days until it was over. Internally, I was debating whether or not it was my time to leave Greensboro. I mean a year prior no one would have ever told me that I would be considering leaving Greensboro a year later. I mean we had jumped from third to first in food deserts, our project had gained national recognition, and money was finally starting to flow in. It was like the entire year was slowing becoming clear that maybe my project was wanted, but it sure felt like they could do without me.

I was tired of the fakeness and I was tired of the deceit. So I was mainly a mute for the last few markets; only speaking to customers and others when it was absolutely necessary. I had also forgone all newspaper interviews and television appearances except for anything Sho Smoove asked for, and he had reached the level that he was now both on the radio and a news anchor on television (super proud of you bro). But God was making me feel uncomfortable for a reason. In the meantime, I was still working on this book, adding more content and meeting more people who would tell me about my dad.

Ironically the month of November I would meet two gentlemen who would forever change the narrative of my father to me. One was a childhood friend who I ran into one day in the streets. He looked at me and seeing me for the first time in over ten years, he just started to cry. He hugged me, but he was in a rush so he gave me his number and looked me in my eyes and said, "your father didn't kill himself." It was the first time someone had ever told me that. I was stoned faced and didn't know how to respond. He instructed me to call him later that week, and I did.

On the phone, he explained to me that my dad was working on a development project with the former Governor Jim Hunt and would have had no intentions of killing himself. He told me in his hearts of hearts, my father, legitimately either accidentally overdose or somebody had something to do with it. He went on to tell me that certain people were interested in getting my father out of the way. It was people who I would have never thought of. But the veil was being lifted. All of my paranoia was justified in the sense that there was a group of people in the city who intended to the best of their ability to not allow me to reach the heights of my father. He also told me a few urban legends about my dad hiding a big stash of money somewhere around the city, some real folk lore stuff. It was a lot of information to process, but nothing compared to the next friend I met.

The next friend I met I remembered well from my childhood. He ran a barbecue business and he and my father had plans of opening up one of their own. Ironically, I was attending my homecoming at NCCU and ran into him. He had asked me if I had time to sit down and talk, and he proceeded to take me and my lady to a small bar. While we were there, we talked and reminisced about my dad. He paused and looked at me and stumbled over his words but what came out was, "I think you need to know the truth." To the best of my knowledge, I thought I knew the truth or at least the allegations in details He looked in my eyes and said, "you know your dad was one of my best friends, but your dad was bisexual."

You can imagine how in shock I was to hear him say that to me. I mean it was almost like my world was turned upside down in an instant. I must admit, I was not as angry as I imagined I would be. If anything, I was upset that it was almost like everyone knew except me, and that was the case. He then asked me if I remembered a phone in the back of my dad's Benz which is almost confirmation that I knew he wasn't lying because very few people knew my dad kept a phone in the trunk of his car. I never seen him take it out. I was rambling in his trunk one day and stumbled across it.

Although I never asked what it was for, the friend told me that that was almost his bat line into this lifestyle. He went on to deny ever having sex with my dad, but told me he knew a few of my dad associates in that lifestyle. Most of them were predominant preachers. He went on to promise me to take me to Atlanta to meet one of them, and he ensured me that my mouth would hit the floor once I saw who it was. I am still waiting for that meeting. He went on to tell me to not be ashamed of my dad's past because they were my father's decisions and that they honestly didn't have anything to do with me, and he was correct. My father was still a great father to me. He went told me how many people owed my father favors for what he had done for them, and that it was my time to collect. In hindsight that information he provided to me was freedom money couldn't buy. The truth really will set you free.

Now let's talk about the word bisexual. To me and with the very reliable sources I spoke to about my dad on the subject, this act was a lot about power. That's where most of the sexual gratification occurs. I spoke to my Uncle about what I had learned, and I believe as his son and as his older brother we only desired to understand why. We had long deep discussions about my father and his upbringing. How him not growing up in the presence of his mother affected him and how my grandfather did not do her best in showing my father the love he needed. Tough love, in turn, is all he got.

My uncle and I narrowed it down to either be between the time my dad left Catholic school and the time he finished wrestling in which an incident had to occur. Although my dad disclosed the fact that he was molested as a child, little detail is known when and where. My uncle started his own child molestation prevention program that he had no intentions of using as a platform to talk about his brother, but it's funny how God can set your course to a re-route for his purpose. And now, we both are able to use my father's story as a means to protect children while they are young so that unnatural sexual cravings as a child can be prevented before it gets defined and refined over time. Now the only thing that I was told that my dad participated in was mutual masturbation and that was enough for me.

I'm sure some people would say that's all it was, and I'm sure some people would say there was more to the story. To me, it's neither here nor there because it is more so the desire to want to do any of that stuff that I would consider bisexual. But I can't and won't demonize my father. He had his demons and I have mine. I am not bisexual, but I will no longer allow that to be the totality of my father's legacy because my father was a good man who loved his children. I left those two experiences with a totally new appreciation for my father. As an adult now it was easier for me to deal with my own demons.

The mobile market finally ended, and I finally felt a little burden lift off my shoulders. I started to feel the urge to leave Greensboro much more. I reached back to the UVI, and they told me that the program did not start until August which worked out for me because after Mr. Valee heard about my intentions, we immediately starting planning for an outdoor operation in the Virgin Islands. It was time to say goodbye to Greensboro.

The final steering committee meeting was scheduled that Friday. During the meeting, I was abnormally quiet. The itinerary items addressed future plans and intentions, but I provided no input. Finally one of the steering members asked if anyone had anything else to say before we dismissed, and that's when I finally spoke up and announced that I was leaving for St. Thomas. It got so silent in the room that you that you could hear rat piss on cotton. The room echoed in silence.

I look over to one of the members Mr. Barnhill, and he

had a slick grin on his face. I could tell he was proud of me. Then Mrs. A hit me in the arm and said, "MATT!" I could tell she really was sincerely upset I was leaving. Everybody else seemed sad, but who knows. It felt good though; not because I was leaving the steering committee, but to know that I was able to close this particular chapter in my life. That evening the first person hit me up about the article, fitting enough, was Robbie Perkins. He told me that he knew some people in Greensboro would be kicking themselves after they read it. I thanked him for his continued support, but felt weird because usually when a newspaper article comes out about me everybody at least texts me to say, "Hey I saw you in the paper." He was the first person to say something, and it was already six so I figured nobody read the article which was fine with me because it was more so for me, anyway.

The very next morning I got a called from Jerry Blackwell and I mentioned to him my article had come out. He asked me to send it to him. I sent him the link. And he posted it on Facebook. I don't know if it's because we had so many mutual friends or that people just decided to wait until Monday to read my article but for the next three days, my phone rang off the hook with support. I got essays, long messages from people telling me about how inspired my story was and encouraged me to keep striving. I mean; my mom's friends, my dad's friends, old church members, and people I had not talked to since second grade. Everyone seemed so proud of me in a sophisticated way. I embraced my new found cheering team of supporters, and I told myself that it was time for The Everybody Eats Company to make its mark in the world.

CONCLUSION- Love Yourz

For what's money without happiness?
Or hard times without the people you love
Though I'm not sure what's about to happen next
I asked for strength from the Lord up above
Cause I've been strong so far
But I can feel my grip loosening
Quick, do something before you lose it for good
Get it back and use it for good
And touch the people how you did like before
I'm tired of living with demons
Cause they always inviting more

-J. Cole Love Yourz

My daughter's health has been steadily improving. Having sickle cell is a heavy burden to deal with, and I am thankful that her mother is such a great mom. My daughter has been the constant driving force behind my determination to succeed. I want to be able to provide all the opportunities that my parents provided for me, and although I did not have her under the best circumstances, she is what I like to call my gift from above.

My goal is to obtain the wealth needed to fulfill my purpose and not a penny more. In a lot of ways, I feel as if I am a top draft pick in the realm of business. I have all the potential in the world and everybody is waiting for me to perform. At that point, I was forced to start thinking of the many options I could use to set myself up for my for-profit. That way I wouldn't succumb to the same allegations that were brought against my dad in doing my nonprofit work. As the scriptures say God always has a ram in the bush.

I have been doing a lot of public speaking to inform and educate people on food deserts and how my company could be the solution to a global problem. I found that I have a passion for public speaking and it is probably the result of being the son of a preacher. College provided me with many platforms to practice speaking in front of crowds. The hardest question growing up for me to answer was, what were my talents? I didn't think I was talented in any particular thing. I was just fairly good at a few things, but I found my talent in public speaking. It gives me certain rush and sense of accomplishment after every public speaking event I attend.

I always get compliments on how well spoken I am. I am always humbled by those who tell me they enjoy hearing me speak especially kids. If I can tell my story to just one child that will help them make a better decision about anything in life, then I know I did the right thing. I have come to a peace about my father's legacy. Even if there isn't ever a formal acknowledgment of what he contributed to the world, I see his prints everywhere I look especially when I look in the mirror. I didn't do it for the pleasure of anyone else, but it was more so therapeutic for me. Lastly, I just would like to address my dad directly…

I wrote him a letter…

Dear Dad,

Well, let me start this off by saying, "I love and I miss you more and more each day." I really want you to know how hard it has been without you. Not from anything in particular, but life itself. Just waking up knowing that my Superman isn't physically here still hurt. I remember every night before going to bed calling 336-255-0238. Sometimes I still dial the number on the phone wishing to hear your voice on the other line.

I miss our motorcycle rides, jet ski rides, fishing, riding horses, eating sugar cane, letting me stay up late on Sunday night to watch pay-per-view WWF or WCW. I remember because of your busy schedule you would only make a few of my games, but I never held it against you. When you did come, it made me want to play harder because my dad was there to see me. I wish most people could understand the fact that I was too young to really understand what you understood as a businessman, but I totally understood who you were as a pastor, but Jesus didn't spend that much time in church. The Bible says so (laugh out loud). With that being said, I remember how many people came to you with their problems and issues. I wish people could understand how many people's lives you affected and how many people you helped.

Because you helped so many people, it rubbed off on me. You taught me how to help people in need. You taught me to take pride in my work and that doing good and well at the same time is the only option for true success. I am taken back when I think about what you truly accomplished in your time with only a high school degree. I wish people understood that you were dyslexic, and that you were insecure about yourself around people who had college degrees; even if they worked for you. I wish people understood the fact that you were molested as a child and was estranged from your mom just like I was estranged from my mom. I wish they understood that a lot of your business intelligence contributed to the fact that your father put you in charge of his businesses when you were 13. I wish they knew that your temper in the business arena was just your defensive way to compensate for not having what you thought was needed (credentials) in order to be accepted among your peers.

Why don't they understand the impact that you made on Greensboro and give you your credit for the property tax base they still enjoy gathering revenue from years later? I always had this strange understanding of your business side; guess that was the King in me. I just kind of wish you would have seen that I was the business son and that Malachi's gift really is music. I think he now has PTSD from not being allowed to do music for so long that he doesn't know what to do with it, and that nothing is holding him back but himself. I tried to break the generational curse in that sense because for the life of me, I can't understand why you and Uncle Ray didn't come up with million dollar ideas. I guess he and I are trying to make up for lost time now Bethany is going to be an amazing business woman too if she can just stay focus, but I know she misses you a lot. I just want you to know it was really hard after you left. Really hard.

And I get so frustrated with you and momma, like why even charter my path if you two were going to abandon me? But I still feel your presence around me. I wish I could just talk to you one more time; there is so much I want to say, so much I want to ask. Like how did you know Thomas? Do you or anybody understand the influence Ward had on you and the manipulation that was placed on your childhood experience of being molested? Why attempt suicide so many times? Could it be you never really wanted to do it, but rather was just using it as a means to cry out for help? What if they found out it was never your intention to kill yourself? What if they knew that you often forgot whether you took your medicine or not and would often come and ask us if you had taken it? What if they would have reported the fact that the microwave blew up, and that it would be mighty strange for a person planning to kill themselves to put some food in the microwave as they are in these final moments… right?

What if they found out that you were in the middle of closing a development deal with former Governor Hunt and according to sources close to the situation claimed that you were excited about the deal…. strange right? What if they found out that you knew you were not going to be criminally convicted of any wrongdoing? What if they found out that it was some people who wanted you out of the way… permanently. That you were in the middle of a hostile takeover of Greensboro business wise, almost becoming untouchable… that would be crazy right? Why as a pastor would you preach from one bible, but then have such an extensive library beyond the bible at home?

Could it be because you believed that there was more to the story of Jesus that you did not preach about on Sunday? Was that what the "fellowship" was all about? And finally, why don't these people know about the story of Moses and Joshua? Why don't they understand that the same God that took Michael King from Dudley SGA President to Dr. Michael King with no college degree has already granted the honor of having my B.A & M.S., and at 27 will be enrolling into a doctoral program. Just like you, just in a different fashion and a little younger…that's crazy right?

I wish you could see your granddaughter Faith. She would have definitely melted your heart and had you wrapped around her finger. I only ask you speak to your wife and encourage her to have a relationship with your granddaughter for the both of you. Continue to look after me as I look forward to the day of reuniting with you. I can count on my hands how many times you have come to me in my dreams and you seem so at peace. Based on how my life is going, it's obvious you are up there Michael King-ing my situations from the heavens.

I love you Pop with every fiber of my being. I love you, and I hope you are proud of me.

Sincerely,
Your Yellow Boy

As I once said in an interview, I feel as if my faith has been tested so much I'm at the point where I can't fail. I now understand the difference between failing and failure–for failure is only the opportunity to begin again more intelligently. I hope my words encourage you to look past your personal circumstances. The Bible says, "No weapon formed against you shall prosper." It never said the weapon wouldn't be formed. The moral of the story is no matter how big the obstacle or how bad the circumstance everything is going to work out, and if it hasn't worked out… keep working!!

This book is a book for dreamers anybody who has ever dreamed of something big. Embody the fortitude to get up and turn your dreams into your reality. Nobody said it would be easy, but take it from me, it's worth it! And as J. Cole said "Gotta be careful what you wish for… as you can see things change."

I wanted to tell the story of someone who has rolled with the punches of life to attempt to make something out of the scraps I was left. I titled this book, "Test of Man." This was a poem that I learned while I was joining my fraternity; the poem goes like this….

"The test of a man is the fight that he makes.
The grit that he daily shows
The way that he stands upon his feet
And takes life's numerous bumps and blows.
A coward can smile when there's nothing to fear and nothing his progress bars. But it takes a man to stand and cheer while the other fellow stares. It isn't the victory after all. But, the fight

a brother makes. A man when driven against the wall, takes the blows of fate, with his head held high bleeding, bruised, and pale!! It Is the man who will win, fate defy. For he isn't afraid to fail."

-Test of a Man

...Jah Bless!!!
-Matthew "Prince" King, M.S. (Future Ph.D)

Meet The Author

Matthew has established himself as an entrepreneur, speaker, scholar, and community servant. He was the Co-founder, and Executive Director of Vision Tree Community Development Corporation (VTCDC). Matthew was also the CEO of Triad Food Hub, a company that connects local farmers with local retail demand. After graduating from Northeast Guilford High School, Matthew enrolled at North Carolina Central University (NCCU), where he earned a B.S. in History. While attending NCCU, Matthew was an active member in the Student Body Association, holding titles such as Mr. Freshman and special assistant to the Student Body President. Matthew also began developing his public speaking skills while hosting numerous educational and social events during his time on campus and off campus. Matthew is also a proud member of Alpha Phi Alpha Fraternity Inc. He was an intern under Dr. Andrea Harris at the North Carolina Institute of Minority Economic Development for two years.

During an internship in 2011, Matthew was introduced to Urban Farmer Will Allen and had the idea to create a business venture around his "Growing Power" urban agriculture model. Two years later, Matthew has been published in numerous publications including the News and Record, and the Winston-Salem Journal. He has been seen on numerous local news station channels and television shows for his enterprising efforts around food including Shark Tank.

After Graduation in spring 2013, Matthew moved back to Greensboro and enrolled into North Carolina A&T State University and earned a M.S. in Agriculture Education in spring 2015. Triad Food Hub was re-branded into The Everybody Eats Company, and in spring 2015 Matthew won NCIMED's Young Entrepreneur of the year. He is currently located in St. Thomas Virgin Islands getting his PhD in Creative Leadership and Innovation at the University of the Virgin Islands. He will also be a proud three time graduate of HBCU's. His focus is hydroponics, aquaponics, and aquaculture. He has relocated to one of the meccas of commercial density farming here in the Virgin Islands teaching high school aquaponics at Eudora Kean.

Matthew is the son of late Dr. Michael and Charles Etta King. He has an older brother Malachi, younger sister Bethany, and a beautiful 6-year-old daughter Faith and spouse Angelica.

For booking information or volume book order please email your inquiry to HearPrinceKingSpeak@gmail.com

ACKNOWLEDGEMENTS

Special thanks to Tyrone James, Roddick Howell, and Greg Hill for the help and support to make this project happen.

My Everybody Eats Family, thank you for your support. I know I am a very difficult person to work with at times, but I appreciate every last one of you. Let's get ready to do great work!!

J. Cole, sounds odd because I never met you, but your music became the soundtrack to my journey and I thank God for the vessel your music has provided me. In a strange way, I always felt like your music filled the void to having my brother Malachi locked up. Any time I need big brother advice I usually type your name in the YouTube search bar. And please if you, Mr. Carter, and the other hip hop greats can refrain from suing me for using you guys' lyrics in this book that would be great.

To my Vision Tree Board, Shawn, Terriss, Shalonda, Faith, and Pastor Graves; thank you guys for believing in me. Your support and guidance has made me a better businessman and without you guys, I would have never made it to this stage. I love each one of you dearly, thank you.

To my family, I thank you guys for your continued support and prayers. To the King, Beasley Family, Henry Family, Coffey Family, Bynum Family, Hall Family, Cleveland Family, Hedgepeth family; thank you guys for making me family. To my Eggerson family in Memphis, I love you guys. Thank you for always making Memphis home especially Auntie Laura, Auntie Shell, Auntie Gwen, Jr & Tricy, and the entire family. To the younger generation of my family, it's our time… let's set the bar high. La Familia forever!

To my two angels, it hurts my heart to think that both of you had your lives cut short. I knew both of you since birth It's still surreal to think that you two are gone. But please continue to look after me, and the family loves you both Tamia and Chekeria.

To the village that raised me. The "Norf" (North) side of Greensboro will forever be in my heart like my bro Calvin says, "We come from a place where loyalty means something."

To the two people who probably would never expect their names to be in this section; Thomas and Aleshia. I thank God for the both of you. I don't know if I would have ever made it to this chapter of my life as fast if it wasn't for the fact that God used you two as a vessel to opposite and challenge my spirit. So, for all the hell you two provided me over the years, Thank You. Aleshia, I sincerely thank you for raising our daughter to the best of your ability, and I only wish you could see that I love her just as much as you do. I am honored to share parenthood with you. Although it has not been the easiest, I hope you understand the sacrifices I have made to provide Faith the best future possible just as I recognize your sacrifices. Contrary to your belief, I think you are an amazing woman and we have shared many laughs in the past, and that is what I will choose to focus on from here on out. I wish you all the best. Thomas, I thank you for showing me what a man is NOT supposed to be, and although you could not show me how to be a man, your example of less than one was example enough. Again, I thank you both.

To my siblings Malachi and Bethany, God could not have blessed us with a better upbringing and now it is upon us to get our family legacy alive. Beth, I am so proud of the woman you have evolved into and I know daddy is proud as well. You are one of the strongest people I know and through all of our trials and hell God has blessed you with daddy's sense of humor that always allows for you to bring a smile to my face in the most difficult of times. I love you with all my heart baby girl you know big bro will go to the ends of the universe and back for you.

Malachi, well first off, you still owe me a car; but beyond that I know as a man I am not sure I could have survived the things that you have lived and that is all Glory to God because boy you a fool (laugh out loud). You are also the most talented person that I know personally, and I pray that this time has served you well to focus your attention on your dreams and that it has given you the courage to chase your dreams with reckless abandon. I was your biggest fan, and I am still your biggest fan. I can't wait until you get home. Hold your head high. I love you, bro.

To my mother, I know we have been on this roller coaster for a while but I pray for your healing. I pray that men never abandon or mistreat you again. I pray that you remember that the only man who never would is, me. I just want you to be my mother again. You are the only one who can fix the title of this book, Love Matte-o

To my wife to be Angelica. I can't formulate the words to articulate what you mean to me so I won't try. I'll simply say I thank you for sticking by my side through the thick and thin. I would also like to thank your mom and your family for their support. This is only the beginning momma bear, I love You.

To my daughter, I pray that this book provides you peace over the years to know that both of your parents sincerely love you and that your father is willing to go to the ends of the world and back for you. As I work to be a better father, I pray for your forgiveness for me not being in the house thus far in your life. I will use the rest of my life attempting to make up for our time lost but our relationship will continue to grow and I can't wait to see the beautiful soul inside of you develop. I love you with all my heart Faith.

Made in the USA
Columbia, SC
11 January 2021

30676642R00133